# Look at You

**Essentials for taking good care of yourself and relationships.**

**by**

**Dr. Larry D. Williams**

*CID, Inc.*
*1225 E. Beltline Rd.*
*DeSoto, Tx. 75115*



*Published by arrangement with*
*Advanced Concept Design Books, a division of*
*CID, Inc. Tx*
*Library of Congress Control Number*
*to be assigned*
*International Standard Book Number*
*ISBN 13: 978-0-9799723-4-8*
***ISBN 10: 0-9799723-4-5***



*For information, address*

***Dr. Larry D. Williams***
***12800 Hillcrest Rd.***
***Suite A 224***
***Dallas, TX 75230***
***972-980-9111***
***ldwilliams@advancedconceptdesign.com***

*First paperback printing* ***September 2008***
*Printed in the United States of America*

# ACKNOWLEDGEMENTS

I have been working on this book over a period of years. So many wonderful people have contributed. Major influences on my work were Dr. Kenneth Pepper, Dr. Harvey Davission, Dr. John Newport and Dr. Joseph Zinker.

I have also learned volumes from hundreds of clients through my practice. One major support was Mike Tatum, a dear friend. His encouragement, bantering of ideas and vivid illustrations played a major role. Mike died in 1998, a major loss to all who knew him.

I am very grateful to my college professor, Betty McCommas, whose encouragement allowed me to reach a level of education in order to write this book. Betty also read and made necessary corrections.

My secretary of over 35 years, Charlene Reedy, provided valuable help in typing making corrections, and offering suggestions. A deep gratitude goes to her.

Others who have rendered help deserve to be mentioned and thanked are Jean Gold, Sue Bravenec, Dani Rouse and Lynn Woods.

My ultimate appreciation goes to my lovely wife, Linda, whose presence and support contribute to all that I do.

## TABLE OF CONTENTS

# INTRODUCTION

Self-love and self-care are essential to a quality life. Through over 30 years of helping people as a psychotherapist, I have observed a clear pattern.

People who come to me for help have neglected their own needs. They have had various difficulties most of their lives. Either they have condemned themselves or blamed others or both.

The helplessness they feel has led to depression, anxiety, and broken relationships. Having been taught that their conscience should be their guide they now feel unending condemnation. As children they learned to point the finger of blame for their unhappiness at others but that requires others to change before you can be happy which never works. The simple truth is that our conscience is a recording of those who raised us, and can be revised by an act of our will. You can be very happy with life without a single change in someone else. However, these truths can be extremely difficult to accomplish.

Because change is so difficult, I guide you to look for internal resources that you can draw upon to achieve an enjoyable life. Getting to these resources involves self-discovery, working through painful obstacles, forgiving yourself and others, and moving forward with hope and determination. In order to do this, you need the cooperation of all your sub-personalities or ego states. In this book, I direct you to love and care for yourself.

Because life's difficulties start in childhood, understanding your memories as a child is the key to communicating with yourself. Healing requires a conversation between you now and the child stored in your recorded memory.

In this book, I have utilized the most basic model of the human experience – "the family" as a method of developing a fuller life. The universal longing for father's and mother's blessing can now be fulfilled. Your personality includes a mother-type and a father-type that can do the blessing. I discuss ways to find them, develop them, and create an internal family. Instead of feeling pulled apart, you will feel a coming together. The healing you need is within you.

In chapter one, I address the confusions often felt between what feelings tell us and what thinking tells us. If our thoughts and feelings stay in conflict over a period of time, we become depressed. Without harmony between them, we cannot live in peace. I also show how sub-personalities or ego states easily translate into family metaphors. By assigning roles to our inner voices, it is easier to identify and relate.

In the next chapter, I talk about parents and growing up. Learning the difference between good parenting and bad parenting is essential to re-interpreting childhood. I point out the importance of relating as an adult to your parents.

I examine the reason we often return to our childhood feelings in chapter three. Everyone regresses to a child likeness at times. With an understanding of how regression works, you can identify when it happens and take measures to give yourself necessary attention. The past is gone forever, nevertheless when the recorded memory of the past plays, the feelings come back. Though the events of the past cannot be changed, the interpretation of the events can be. This chapter points out ways to make those changes happen and bring about peace and healing.

Chapter four describes the mother within the personality. The mother function is essential throughout life. Identifying the inner mother is only the beginning of self-discovery. Understanding the distinctive functions and putting them into operation is essential. We will always need a mother and the only way to achieve that is to mother ourselves. The attributes of being tender, encouraging, affirming, and loving unconditionally makes life good.

The fathering role is covered in the fifth chapter. If you did not have good fathering and you do not compensate, you will suffer your entire life. When you reach adulthood you have to take charge, make decisions, and be responsible. You must be strong, committed, confident, courageous and the list goes on. With these attributes, you can face anything!

The inner family encountering life's problems is covered in the next chapter. People face the same problems the world over. Everyone experiences pain, grief, depression, anxiety, and a host of other emotions. We all know illness, accidents, and financial stress (even the rich.) I offer help with issues related to oneself such as self-esteem, self-discipline, self-abuse, and self-forgiveness.

Perhaps the biggest challenge in life is death - the pain of losing friends, relatives, and pets. Then there is our own death to consider.

In the final chapter , I carry internal relationships outside to others. The internal process repeats itself in nearly all relationships. For example, regression can play a significant role. Our level of self-care will play out either in our dependency upon or our contributions to others. How and what we communicate shapes relationships. And the profound significance of loving and being loved, calls for special attention.

In this book, I offer you a method of identifying your inner mother and father and child, not as a simple solution to complex problems, but as a practical approach to something that will help make life better for you amidst confusion, problems, and struggles of everyday life.

Life is suppose to work. If it is not working for you, that does not mean you should never have been born, or that you are no good, or that your circumstance in life cannot be changed. Since you're already here, you are supposed to be here and have purpose and meaning in your life. As a person, you carry the same value as all other people, and as long as you are alive, if you want change for the better is always possible.

# CHAPTER 1: TAKING CARE OF OUR FEELINGS, AND LETTING OUR FEELINGS TAKE CARE OF US.

## I – The Family Within

The relationship between our thinking and our feelings determines the quality of our lives. To make decisions based on logic alone has no joy or spontaneity. To feel without thoughtful guidance has no protection or security. Thinking and feeling need each other. Being close to our feelings and allowing our feelings to inform us, as well as to provide us with play and pleasure, creates a loving intimacy that makes life full and fun.

Life can become very complicated. There are more than 100 billion cells comprising the brain, which has never been fully explored, making it difficult to fathom the complexity of living. It helps however, to maintain a simple approach especially when dealing with the child we once were whose feelings still affect us so deeply every day. So, I have found it is useful to think of ourselves as families, made up of a mother-self, a father-self, and a child-self. All three can think and love and feel, but it helps to assign distinct roles to each. Simply put, the inner parents oversee the inner child and the inner child provides playfulness and feeling insight. As such each serves as a reality check on the other. If our inner family is in discord, we feel awful. If it's in harmony, so are we.

Intelligence comes from both our feelings and our thoughts, and how they inter-relate. Interacting with our feelings involves more than a rational process alone. It must include the intimacy found in good parenting. Since our current feelings can draw on the memory of every past feeling we have ever felt, there is child-likeness about feelings. Therefore, taking care of our feelings is similar to taking care of a child. Skillfully and lovingly parenting ourselves means that our feelings are well taken care of. It feels good.

This capacity for self-parenting is within us from birth. A client told me about his son, Scott, only two years old, who saw his father sitting on the sofa crying because several things in his life had gone wrong. Immediately, little Scott climbed up into his father's lap, began wiping the tears from his cheeks, put his arms around his neck and patted him on the back saying. "Okay, Daddy. Daddy, okay." Scott had already begun to develop the skills of parenting.

Babies arrive with internal capacities for mothering and fathering. The parental role is to help children develop their own parents. A daddy teaching self-daddying so that the child will grow up meeting his/ her own daddy needs. Likewise a mother will teach her child to provide her own mothering needs.

So that when each parent aligns with his/her corresponding likeness within the child, and helps that "likeness" to develop, the child will mature to a level of self-care that provides security, direction, and all other grownup needs.

It would follow that a mother would teach her child not to be harsh, rather to treat himself gently instead. A father may teach his child to be physically tough through typical male activities. The intent is not to create stereotypes by saying that a father can not teach gentleness and a mother can not teach toughness. Rather I am referring to physical tendencies in traditional roles. A parent, male or female, who learns to model both roles, will be more balanced and a better role model to his or her children. Androgyny which is both male and female in each person provides the best balance for life.

As the child is cared for and taught to care for himself, eventually his parents are no longer needed. In fact, the role of parents is to teach their children not to need them. For example, teaching a child to tie his own shoes frees parents from that responsibility. A child who never learns to tie his own shoes will spend his life either stepping on his shoelaces, or expecting someone else to tie them for him. Even worse would be the child's inability to tie his own emotional shoes.

The ability to fully provide for our emotional needs frees us from unhealthy dependency on parents and others. Freedom to make our own choices is the condition necessary for our ability to love. Therefore, our quality of life is dependent on the skilled inner parents within us who lovingly care for our inner child, as well as on our inner child who can feel safe, secure and trusting enough to live and love and play.

Although the inner mother and father reach maturity, it is important to remember that the inner child never grows up. All the memories, feelings, events, experiences, thoughts and fantasies from every age remain intact. Daily events enter through the five senses to stimulate

the memories. The child adds new
and can alter feelings and, thereby,
can mature. But our past is recorded in our subconscious mind and remains an influence on our lives as long as we live. Since it can't truly be forgotten, it can only be suppressed or dealt with.

## II - When the System Breaks Down

When our inner parents fail to develop, the result is a child in an adult body. Children will put on their parents' clothes and play grown-up roles, but for some the drama continues long after they are grown. This poses a serious problem because the inner child can never become an adult. Only the inner parents develop to be adults.

A child in an adult body was the theme of the movie, "Big", which was a metaphor for a vast number of people whose inner parents never matured. Failure to attain the adult parent position is demonstrated in three types of behavior: Good Actors, Orphans, and Average Strugglers.

### The Good Actors

One group with undeveloped inner

parents is the good actors, who are usually hard to recognize. These are people who may be leaders in companies and governments. They look mature because they act confident, but in some or many ways they are small children dressed in adult clothes, afraid of being found out.

Throughout history nearly every United States president has shown some childishness in his behavior. George Washington was afraid to be emotionally close to people. Franklin D. Roosevelt and John F. Kennedy, as well as several other presidents, needed the approval of women due to a lack of self-mothering. President Johnson had temper tantrums; Nixon played "King of the Hill." The child is alive and well in us all and requires parenting.

The good actors are to be found everywhere. It would be alarming to know how many people who perform adult roles; teachers, preachers, lawyers, pilots, doctors, soldiers go home at the end of the day and shake with fear. And their families could tell you unbelievable stories about their immature behavior.

## The Orphans

Another group is the orphan group. Their inner parents have not developed and their inner child feels abandoned. Unable to imitate adult behavior, they cannot cope; consequently, they seek adoption. Their newspaper ad would read:

**Parents Wanted**

"Wanted: Parents to take care of me. I need parents to see that I have a good place to live, clothing, food, and toys. I want parents who will encourage, and be nice to me, give me direction, and be proud of me. I want parents to provide me with security, and happiness. Someone *please* adopt me; am only forty-five years of age. Phone: 123-HELP"

It sounds rather ridiculous for a forty-five year old to apply for someone to adopt him. Unbelievable as such an ad might be, I had a thirty-five year old client tell me recently, in all excitement, "I've found a woman who is willing to be my mother. She has agreed to legally adopt me."

Stunned I replied, "You don't need someone to adopt you," "You have a mother inside you who's all the mother you need - and you can learn to be the kind of mother you've always wanted. That inner self-mother is the only one who can ever really mother you - the only one who'll always be with you." The internet has created a quest for outside help beyond anything we could have imagined.

Elvis Presley's special need for his mother was not due to a little boy inside him who never grew up, but to a mothering capacity inside him which failed to mature. He did not know how to take care of his little boy needs. In his crippled condition, he kept seeking mother's approval and blessing. He was lost without her. His greatest achievement was to make her happy because doing so would gain her attention and nurturing. When his mother died, he sought substitutes to mother him. He wanted Priscilla to give him what he needed from his mother, but she could not. He sought happiness in the attentions and approval of many women. Probably no man in history received more attention and approval from women than Elvis, but he remained unhappy because no one could provide for him the love, acceptance, care, protection, and nurturing he was unable to provide for himself.

Others look for a father. Some women marry a certain type man because they need a father. Church members may blindly follow their pastor as obedient children do their father. In more extreme cases some look to gurus, or cult leaders like Jim Jones, dedicating themselves wholly to these demagogues as father substitutes. They follow a "Hitler" without question, because they want a daddy. The intense need for a father to oversee them is simply the result of an undeveloped father inside themselves.

All of us need a mother and father. Either we can find them within our own personality or we will embark on a futile external search for them. Seeking others to parent us is sure to fail. No overseer, other than our parents within, can adequately take care of us. No one else can be with us twenty-four hours a day, know our deepest emotions, and have the freedom from their own needs to be able to give us undivided attention. After our childhood years, whether we've been prepared for it or not, the parenting job belongs to us and all attempts to escape or avoid it are assured to bring us some measure of pain.

## The Average Strugglers

A third group might be referred to as the average strugglers. These people have partially developed parent-selves which means that at times their inner parents fail to come through and the child flounders. After a time, they regain confidence and their child feels secure again. Eventually, they repeat the damaging process.

Most of us can identify with this group since there are no perfect parents or perfect people. Most of my clients come from this group. The good actors have deceived themselves into believing their own performance and believe therapy would be a put down to their performance. The orphans sometimes seek therapy but many are trapped into the neurotic notion that their only hope is to find someone who will take care of them. A lot of average strugglers seek help.

## III - Essential Steps Toward Taking Care of Yourself

The answer is not to better develop the child's performance. This is what advice givers try to get you to do. The answer is not to find a rescuer, this creates a dependency that is crippling and doomed to fail. Obviously one needs to complete the development of the inner parents, which failed to happen as we grew up.

1. Start by focusing on the distinction between your parent-self and your child-self.
   **Note**: For some people this is easy, but for others it is extremely difficult.

2. Create a dialog between your parent(s)-self and your child-self.

3. Educate your inner parents on good parenting skills.

4. You may need to rescue your child from a painful past - and you can do that.

5. Develop a daily schedule that includes unique ways of acknowledging that wondrous and worthy self-child within

> you: Special sharing time - the kinds of loving discussions you've always wanted; activities that include both your parent-self and the child-self. This book is designed to help you understand and implement this process of self-love and care.

When Bob came to me for the first time he was consumed with tremendous fear and trembling. He worked in city government, and was in charge of overseeing several citywide operations as well as involved in state legislative activity. He was nervous and shaky as he said to me, "I am just so frightened."

"Maybe that's because you're trying to make the little boy in you take responsibility for all the heavy activities you face." I explained, "Let the little boy be free of all that worry, and go play. You have the intelligence and the capacity you need, or you would not have the job." Bob agreed and I appealed to him to trust that and release the little boy from the responsibility and duty of overseeing all the activities.

I suggested that before he went into a council meeting, he take his hand and squeeze his other forearm and say, "Son, I have the knowledge, wisdom, and power to handle this situation. You may go play while I handle adult matters." An unbelievable change occurred. He reported a confidence he had not felt before. That was several months ago, and today he says that the fear is basically gone. This technique, combined with his therapy, has allowed him to feel confident and safe.

Jane came for therapy at age thirty, but emotionally she was still a small scared child. She would consult her mother on most decisions and her husband was more like a father whose instructions she followed. As she developed her own inner parents, those who had previously been parenting her became angry--- a common occurrence. Jane's mother became angry because Jane chose to leave her husband. Even after Jane had gone from her husband, her mother continued to show anger because Jane had not consulted with her before making various decisions.

One technique I have used in therapy is to have a doll made which resembles the client. I made a doll, which looked like Jane as a small child. First, she brought several photos of herself as a little girl. That day we worked on her feelings about the child that she saw in each photograph then selected a photo to use in making the doll. When Jane first saw the doll she cried and held it tightly. With the doll as a symbol of her feelings, she learned to talk to it as she would to her feelings. She was very passionate; caring and nurturing, unlike her previous treatment of her feelings, which had been harsh and judgmental.

During her therapy, Jane had gotten a divorce, rented and furnished an apartment, bought a car, changed jobs, and made many new friends. She came into the office recently and said she was moving. She was very proud of herself, and her newfound freedom and maturity. "You know," she grinned, "I did not call my mother or brother or anyone else, to ask their opinion. I simply held my doll and discussed the matter with her."

A very excited Jane had begun to be in charge of her own life, which came from finding and activating her own mother-self and father-self.

# CHAPTER 2: FROM MOMMY AND DADDY TO ME

To have perfect parents would be a dream come true. Unfortunately, perfect parents, like perfect people, fall into the category of fairy tales and fantasies. There have been no living examples identified and cataloged. My parents were like your parents, they made mistakes. My children can tell you about the mistakes I made. Obviously, some parents are "better" than others, but all are found wanting in some area.

About the only training most of us get in the "how to" of parenting, comes from the example set by our own parents; as a result imperfections are passed from generation to generation. Identifying these flaws is a never-ending process.

## I – Parenting Mistakes Can be Costly

Six year old John was sent to the store by his mother. He went off on his errand, despite some pangs of fear, proud and happy that mom trusted him with a "big person" job. On the way to the store he met an older boy who threatened to beat him up, then took away all his money. John was frightened, angry and humiliated. He ran screaming and sobbing all the way home.

Needing a reassuring word and hug, John told his mother what had happened. She responded by scolding him harshly and critically for losing the money. John was never the same again. The innocence with which he had trusted became severely tarnished.

This experience followed by other failures to be reassured with loving tender care when he was scared, reinforced his fears and left him timid right up to this day. Now, nearly forty years old, he becomes so overwhelmed by a sense of inadequacy and fear of failure he sometimes is afraid to leave his house. For John to overcome his fears, he must alter the effects of what his mother did to him. Change is essential for him to live and grow.

When I was growing up, parents simply were parents. I never thought much about good or bad parents. Oh, we got upset if our parents didn't let us do things, but we never discerned between the good and bad our parents did. My parents were caring, decent, wonderful, God loving people and I loved them very much. Everything they did, or did not do, was with good intentions for us, their children!

Nevertheless, for many years I sought outside

approval because of low self-esteem. At times I'm passive and sometimes I even experience mild depression. Occasionally I'm nervous about sharing my views and especially about defending them. I believe that my mother, father, two brothers and sister experienced some or all of these traits, as well. Once I learned to parent myself, I began to make great strides in my growth in these areas, although sometimes I suffer still.

To oversee the blooming of a child from birth to adulthood is an awesome task. Perfection is hardly possible. I wanted, very much, to be a perfect parent, but at times I reacted too quickly-before I thought!

A medical doctor once returned my phone call seeking advice. I was always nervous talking with doctors. Believing as I grew up that they were "above" me, it was important to me to impress this doctor. While I was talking with him, my three-year-old son picked up the extension and said, "Hi." I humiliated myself by screaming into the phone, "Monte, you hang up that phone right now!" The doctor was Monte's pediatrician, and I imagine I really impressed him! As for Monte - it was difficult to get him to talk on the phone after that. Because of my need to impress the doctor, I behaved in a way that put a scare in my son.

Sometimes we feel driven to parent our children in a way that would make our own parents proud - if our parents were observing us. Even when our parents are deceased, we may say or think, "If my mom (dad) knew I let my child get away with that, she would roll over in the grave."

Whatever methods, poor or otherwise, grandma and grandpa used to raise them, likely these same methods were used by our parents to raise us -- and then by us and on and on.

Some of us rebel against the way we were parented - and go to extremes in the opposite direction. If our parents were too strict, we become too permissive. If they were too permissive, we become heavy-handed. Consequently, the parenting is still flawed, and the children still suffer. There are no perfect parents!

## II - We Want to be Like Our Parents

All children are imitators. They can be counted on to imitate their parents in action, attitude, and behavior complete with imperfections, and all!

When I was a child, I noticed that my father's jaw "popped" as he ate. Fascinated, I tried moving my jaw into many grotesque positions, trying and trying to get it to pop the way his did. Later in life I learned that an alignment problem, combined with taking bites of food that were too large for him to easily chew, made his jaw pop.

The power of the parental model is overwhelming. It is difficult to understand and accept that many a child who was beaten by his parents grows up to beat his own child; or that many children who were molested by their parents grow up and molest their own children. But it does illustrate the power that the parental example has in our own lives and behavior. We want, and as children we need, to envision our parents as OK people so we mimic their behavior in support, to prove that they are valued in spite of what they did.

The way our parents treated us explains a lot about our behavior and feelings. The tone of our voice, our political and religious views, the way we eat, how we handle financial matters, how we settle differences, whether we are passive or assertive, all bear a resemblance to our parents.

When I was a child and a storm blew up, we paid

it little attention, except to close the windows so it would not rain in - even during the summer. Otherwise, we were unimpressed by the violence of the weather. My wife's family, however, reacted much differently. They would become actively involved: listen to weather reports, become tense and alert, and possibly go to the storm cellar. Can you imagine the difference between the way my wife and I react in our home together, during a storm?

Parents are more than people to their children. They are gods. They created us. They provided our home, food, clothes, and health and tended our emotional needs. We would not have survived without them, or someone acting as a parental figure. They are all-powerful and all knowing, and, as with gods we must do their will. Life is made up of choices to obey them or "sin" against them in acts of rebellion. No wonder we grow up to bear their likeness!

Many circumstances are forced on us as children that we may not agree with in our feelings. We may do things that do not feel right to us, giving in and doing them anyway in order to gain parental favor. To avoid our parents' anger we move farther and farther away from our true feelings, when those feelings conflict with our parents' wishes. And, in so doing, we lose contact with our true self.

I heard a little boy in Wal-Mart say, "Daddy, I want that toy." "No, you don't!" his father replied. The father didn't say, "You can't have it." He said, "You don't want it." Does the kid think, "Well, I thought I did," or does he say to himself, "Daddy was wrong, I do want it." When parents continuously undermine a child's decisions, the child does not gain the skill or confidence to manage his feelings and actions himself. A child who is never allowed to tie his own shoes will not be able to keep his shoes on without someone to assist him.

## III – Keeping Family Traditions Alive

An adult who acts irresponsibly is in effect saying that he never learned parental skills, or that he learned faulty ones. Faulty parenting means we treat ourselves with rejection when we need encouragement, or make fun of ourselves when we need strokes, or tell ourselves that people don't like us when in fact they do.

If we were ignored as a child, we likely ignore our own pain, our own needs, and our own desires. If we were condemned as a child, we will use self put-downs about everything we do. If our parents never gave us clear signals as to what they expected of us, we will stay confused in adulthood. If our parents demanded perfection, then we can do no less. If our parents used us or molested us, then such is our role in life to be victims. If our parents were only friends, then we will not know the security of overseeing our lives with authority.

Our attitudes and treatment of our own feelings and behavior will be very much a reflection of the way we were treated as children. When a golfer makes a bad swing and then says to himself, "Can't you do anything right?" he is repeating the words of his parents. When a person stumbles and says, "You clumsy idiot," he is hearing the voice of his parents. When a man punishes himself for a mistake, he is carrying out the will of his parents. Any time we mistreat ourselves, we say, "I want to be just like my mommy and daddy," and the truth is made clear.

Releasing our parents from all responsibility for us is extremely difficult, but very important! No longer needing the security of their money, advice, criticism or approval constitutes a major break. Whether it is the parent or child who refuses to release, making that break can be painful. I lead some of my clients into calling out for their mothers or fathers, over and over again, until they finally break down crying out of the deep need for their parents' love. "Please love me, Mama." "Please love me, Daddy."

The fantasy is, if we were to receive the love and blessing of our parents, everything would then fall into place and we would feel OK about the world and life - in the way we seem to remember feeling when we were children. However, only when we stop seeking or needing the love of our parents and decide to love ourselves, can life feel right.

We can never return to the scene of our childhood. Our age, body size, and the calendar all prohibit us from regaining the comfort and security of childhood with our parents. Oh, yes! We can remember the feeling of being held tenderly by mom or dad. Special holidays, like Christmas or Halloween, may bring memories that cause regression to the feelings of childhood. But, we can never recreate the relationship with our parents that we had as a child. That experience is gone forever. This is one of the most difficult realities for some people to accept.

## IV – Taking Responsibility for Ourselves

The only true parents we have available to us today are the parents inside ourselves. If our inner parents are well taught and have learned to provide for our physical and emotional needs, then all is well. If not, to overcome the way our parents did certain things for us will require a lot of dedication and work.

The child within maintains his childhood memory of mama and daddy. When we talk with our parents, or see them, or look at pictures, those childhood memories come flooding back. Prominent successful adults, when in the presence of their parents, can still be made to feel and act like children.

Frank holds a Ph.D. and manages a department, which includes around 200 people with Ph.D.'s. In the presence of his mother he often reverts to feeling a little boy, again. He gets upset if she disapproves of his behavior and is strongly influenced by her opinion.

Some people judge every move they make, while considering whether or not their parents would approve. Their parents are on their minds often during each day. The continued power of our parents can be staggering. For those adaptive people who always want to please or those rebellious people who set out to do the opposite of what is expected of them, the power of their parents still dominate their lives. They are either seeking their parents' approval or trying to strike back. Parental pleasure or displeasure cannot motivate making changes in life. Healthy change occurs only when we are moved to do what is the best for ourselves, according to our own inner parents.

Relocating the center of power, authority, or pleasure from our outer parents to the parents within us is essential to the realization of our personal worth and freedom. Only then do we gain the capacity to change and improve the way we were parented. Only then can we be parents to ourselves, and acquire the nurturing parents we always wanted.

The parent’s role is to teach their child not to need them; however, sometimes the parent continues to need the child. Doris brought her fourteen-year-old son to see me because he was defiant and locked himself in his room. In my office, the boy kept saying, "I don't want anything to do with you. Stay out of my life." But, she kept insisting that since he was her son he was responsible to relate to her. She had no one else, she said, both he and his sister were her whole life.

When parents fail to find their own place in life, they often seek to find meaning and purpose through their children. They have no real understanding of their own identity or sense of direction, so they attach themselves to their children. This situation poses tremendous guilt for the child, because to release the parents from any parenting responsibilities is to abandon them. Who can be so heartless as to withdraw from a parent who so desperately needs them?

The truth is, by remaining a child to our parents we fail to find our own identity and maturity - and we enable our parents to continue to remain weak. The best we can do for them is to refuse to be their life's purpose. And, thereby, possibly force them to find their own true purpose in life. Sadly, the chance of the latter occurring is very slim, but no matter the outcome, it is not the job of the child to provide purpose in life for his parents - at any age!

Some parents do not know how to parent. They never learned because their own parents never taught them. In fact, bad examples may have been set for them as children, to be repeated by them as adults. Nothing is to be gained by condemning our parents, or grandma and grandpa, because of their lack of parenting skills. This lack does not mean they didn't love or care for us.

Susan sat in my office and cried because her mother had neglected her. She wanted and needed a mother who would be strong, loving, comforting, encouraging and nurturing. Instead, her mother had tried to relate to her as a peer. Mother wanted to share every detail of Susan's life through being Susan's best friend. Even though she meant well by trying to be Susan's pal, Susan was left without a real mother and was angry. Susan's father lived in the home but was unavailable to her. He was a busy professor who took no time out to get close to her. His only function was to make certain requirements of his children. His wisdom, love and trust were unavailable. Now in her late twenties, she still cries for the father she never had. This affects all her current relationships with men.

## V – Understanding Our Parents Love

The basis of feeling loved by our parents will vary for each of us. Every individual looks for certain attitudes and actions that express their parents' blessing of love for them. In order to feel loved one child may need to be touched a lot, another may need to be told, another applauded for his good behavior, still another may need various combinations of all three loving expressions.

Sometimes a child observes the treatment a friend receives from his parents and making comparisons, comes to conclusions about his value to his own parents. For example, if a friend's dad scuffles with him or hunts and goes fishing with him or jokes with him, he may conclude that since his own father does none of these things perhaps his father does not love him. If a girlfriend's Mom tells her how pretty she is, or makes special things for her, or sees that she has nice clothes, but her own mother does none of those things, she may believe that her own mother does not love her.

Many of us feel that our parents either didn't love us enough, or didn't even love us at all. This belief is based on the treatment we received as children. As small children, usually we do not blame our parents, rather we assume that we are unlovable, (thinking, "There must be something wrong with me or I would not be treated this way.")

However, when parents are asked if they love their children all will answer, "Yes!" They may speak of stress factors, work, illness, or lack of ability to communicate, which hinders the expression of their love. Whatever the reasons the damage is done. The child feels unloved.

Judy told me her father loved her but her mother hated her. Her father died during her early teens and since that time she has been in depression because her only hope had been for her father to rescue her from her mother. In fact, she still looks for her father's return to do just that - even though she is now 39 years old.

I believe her mother did love her, but because her mother had emotional problems and drank too heavily, she could not express her love. The consequences, however, are the same as if she did not, in fact, love her child. Judy believed that she was unloved because something was basically wrong with her. Now her self-condemnation has turned to hate for her mother.

Seeking in vain for the approval or blessing which we think will make us happy will eventually cause us to become bitter. Many of us carry inside ourselves, a lot of anger toward our parents. In fact, we may love our parents and hate them at the same time. If we stay stuck in these feelings long enough, depression will emerge. It is extremely important to work through these feelings. This will be explained in greater detail in Chapter 3.

The only way ever to be free is to forgive our parents. Whether they beat, molested, abandoned or put us up for adoption, we will never be free until we forgive them! The energy it takes to condemn them robs us of the energy we need to take care of ourselves. Blame keeps wounds open, only forgiveness heals.
Getting on with our lives, and letting them get on with theirs, is the only way we can ever know our parents. Only after finally accepting them as ordinary human beings can we truly love them again. We can love them because they are valuable people and because of the important role they played in our history. We can love them because of the commonality we share with other relatives. But as long as we need them for approval, security, money, nurturing or any other parental function, we are not free to truly love them.

## VI – Having The Parents We Always Wanted

I bring good news and more good news: I found the parents I've always looked for - and those parents are me!

Making the transition from our childhood parents to our inner parents is not easy. We are hindered by unfinished business with them. We still need their love; we are still angry at them, etc. Or we may feel that, somehow, we are betraying them- we disown them - or perhaps we just don't understand how to make the transition. Whatever the reasons, for many of us it feels easier to remain in the same old rut - feeling like uncared-for children, who keep looking back with regret, or looking around for substitute parents.

Getting acquainted with the child inside, and teaching that child about his inner parents, is a truly exciting experience. As I mentioned in the first chapter, sometimes I ask a client to bring a photograph taken during his infancy or childhood and I have his face, in the photo, transposed onto the face of a doll. During a scheduled session, I introduce him to his inner child as symbolized by the doll. As he holds the doll, I have him say, "I love you, my child, and I'm going to take care of you." The usual emotional response is for my client to burst into tears. This powerful promise from one's inner parents, to provide care for their inner child, is the only real source of protection, nurturing, and love. This creates a special moment of intimacy between parent-self and child-self.

Only faith can bring us to the realization of our inner parents. When we have been separated from our inner parents, neither love from others, success, praise, insight, security, and friends- absolutely nothing-- can make us aware of their presence, except faith. It may be a leap of faith, or a slowly developing trust which grows inside us as we gradually learn that our inner parents are indeed present - and capable of taking care of us.

An underlying self-distrust is often present when we do not feel secure or loved. If we feel our inner parents have betrayed us, trusting ourselves may first require self-forgiveness.

Our inner parents say, "We are sorry we let you down." Our inner child may respond, "I still don't fully trust you, but I forgive you" The relationship begins with a commitment to learn to trust - but healthy trust evolves only through time and work.

When Sally first came to see me she complained that she was often betrayed by her feelings of hurt, fear and sadness. She also complained about her irresponsibility. In the first situation, her inner parents were upset with the inner child. In the latter, her inner child was upset with the overseeing parents.

The first step, in beginning a new relationship between parent and child, is an acknowledgment of the conflict; i.e., the parent and child don't trust each other. Secondly, an initial statement of commitment by the parent, "I will learn how to take care of you. Please forgive me and allow me the chance to learn." The response of the child is "I'm afraid to trust you, but I want to believe you, and I'll work at it." Even though it may feel unnatural, the statement, "I love you," is voiced by the parent to the child and by the child to the parent. Sometimes this brings tears, because each so desperately needs the other.

If we were normal at birth, we have within us the capacity to develop our own set of healthy parents. If we did not have good examples in our childhood parents, then we must find other teachers. Parent models can be found in books, movies, or any source of good information about the parenting role. However, gathering good information, alone, will not work, (any more than acquiring knowledge of swimming will, in itself, make us good swimmers). Our knowledge of good parenting must be combined with the skill of inner communication- i.e., the ability of our inner parents to talk "nurturingly" to our inner child. Without a working dialogue between our inner parent-selves and our inner child-selves, we remain children forever.

Many people have a difficult time talking to children and some, in fact, are even uncomfortable when around children. The child inside each of us, however, is just like all other children, and always will be. A person who cannot relate to the children who come into his life is usually a person who cannot relate to his own child within. By learning to talk to our feelings (our inner child) with interest, care, love, and promise our inner child-feelings will respond in similar fashion.

When I first met Tom, he was contemplating divorce. One issue of conflict was that his wife wanted a child and he did not. He had two children, by a former marriage, who lived in another city and whom he never bothered to contact. He also felt annoyed by the children in his neighborhood. During a therapy session Tom regressed to a time when, as a six-year-old, he was playing in the back yard with his dog. He remembered seeing his parents through the kitchen window, looking at him with what he interpreted as disapproval. Tom left his dog, went into the house and never again played outside with the dog. Life changing meaning can sometimes be adopted by the child through his misperception of his parents' intent.

In fact, Tom never remembers playing again at all. He abandoned his inner child. No wonder he didn't like children! I had him imagine himself returning to the backyard and playing with his dog once again (after learning to deal with his parents' disapproval). He imagined having fun with his dog as he ran and laughed and played.

Tom made contact with his children and went to visit them. He began playing with the neighborhood children and, after a time, decided to remain with his wife and have a baby. Even though they moved to another city, he called to tell me when she became pregnant and called again when the child was born. Both times Tom was bubbling with excitement.

The joy of our inner parent child relationship is found in developing our own interpretation of life, and being free to feel and act as we choose. If we interpret the world as our parents did, we are limited to their thoughts and feelings. In order to become an adult, each child must develop a perspective of life which grows out of his own individuality and experience. This does not mean throwing off all the traditions and values of our parents. We investigate for ourselves and then, after research, consider which truths and values we choose to claim for ourselves. Our own inner mother and inner father decide what is best for us.

## VII – Adopting Your Child

One way to experience the change from external parents to inner parents is to go through an adoption fantasy. In the following scene, I have set up an adoption dialogue, which illustrates how this can be done.

Lisa sat across from me, teary-eyed. "I want you to follow my directions." I said. "Picture in your mind what I am saying. Envision yourself, at your current age, going to visit the home you lived in when you were a small child. You walk to the front door and enter. You see your parents sitting in the front room. Walking past them, you go directly to the room of your child-self (that is, you as a child). You see little Lisa sitting on the bed crying. Tell her you have come to get her, that you are going to take care of her, to provide for her; that you are going to be her parents and she will be with you, safely, from this day forward. Take her by the hand and bring her to you. Raise her up into your arms and hold her, tenderly. Tell her about your love for her; how you have always loved her and how you are going to give her all the comfort, assurance and approval she always wanted. Now begin walking out of the house.

As you go past your parents, tell them, "She doesn't belong to you anymore; she belongs to me. I appreciate what you did to help her and I'll try to correct the things you did wrong. I'm not blaming you at all; it's just that I will now give her all the parenting she wants and needs. So, thank you and goodbye." Walk out of the house and go toward your car, knowing all the while that little Lisa belongs to you now- totally and completely. Adoption is complete. You now have a child to take care of.

She told me later, it was one of the most profound experiences of her life. She could not believe she had taken charge of her own feelings, in the same manner that one adopts a child. She had begun to oversee, provide and care for her feelings in ways she had never done before.

M Tatum

# CHAPTER 3: RETURNING TO YOUR CHILDHOOD FEELINGS

In the movie "Big," a 12-year-old boy has a magic spell put on him, which changes him physically into an adult. While in his adult body he has many exciting experiences, but always he longs to be his real age again. Finally, he manages to get the spell reversed and the camera shows him, walking toward his home, beginning to shrink. By the time he reaches home, he is once again a little boy inside an adult suit, shirt and shoes.

Feeling like a child inside an adult's clothes happens to all of us at one time or another. Everyone regresses, which is to say we feel at times just as we felt when we were younger. A vivid return to the past may be triggered by a song that was played at your high school prom. Perhaps hearing a song you and your sweetheart called "our song" causes you to experience those feelings again.

Memories of the past make us knowledgeable social creatures. In fact, it is those constant recurring memories which allow us to function. How that occurs will be different for each individual. One person may stay regressed or childlike most of the time. Another may seldom contact feelings from the past and even deny these feelings when they do occur. The first person is irresponsible and the second is boring. The rest of us are somewhere between. Coming to understand the process of recurring feelings is one of the most valuable insights we can attain for a peaceful, secure and enjoyable life. In this process lies comprehension of the inner parent-child relationship.

Reliving the painful aspects of our past without a sense of the continual presence today of our inner mother and father, can be frightening. Conversely, selecting the good feelings from our past (warm holiday feelings, for example) with our inner parents as part of our present can be utterly delightful.

## Regression: A Return to (Our) Past

In this chapter I will explain the nature of regression:

1. Regression is stimulated by the five senses: Smell, Sound, Taste, Touch, and Sight.
2. Regression can be subtle: You may be barely aware of what is happening when

earlier feelings overcome you.

3. You may relive good experiences or bad experiences. With time and training you can gain control over this.
4. Regressing can return you to any age: Depending upon how you feel and the external events at the moment, you can go back "one year" or to any stage from your earliest experiences.
5. The regressed child is often confused about the truth: The false notions of childhood frequently come back along with the feelings -- and, since childhood ideas and our adult knowledge don't match we often feel confused.
6. The capacity to handle feelings from the past will vary: This will depend on the intensity of the early feeling, and on your skill at handling these feelings today.

## I - Understanding the Return To Childhood Feeling

### Regression is Stimulated by the Five Senses

There are innumerable causes of regression. Any of the five senses can bring in information that will stimulate memory of thoughts and feelings. For example, the taste of a tootsie roll, eaten again after many years, will place you back in the little neighborhood store, as a child. Or, eating a Popsicle can do the trick. The taste of Christmas candy may return you to the time or feel of a childhood Christmas. The taste of blood from a cut lip may resurrect the less desirable memory of a car wreck you were in. At any rate, there is a strong memory attached to taste, which can make you feel as you did when you were much younger.

Smell is closely aligned with taste; For example, the smell of home fried chicken takes me to grandmothers on Sunday. Once when my parents came to visit me, I walked into the bathroom and there was a strong smell of Colgate toothpaste just like that which I had used as a child and I felt like that child for a moment. The smell of an oak tree takes me, as a child, to the woods of Arkansas. A friend told me that a skunk got under his house and he had to leave for two days. Now whenever he smells a skunk, he returns to that experience.

Sound is a very powerful medium of regression. Everyone can relate to the sudden return to feelings of high school days when he hears a song, which was popular then.

The sound of old music played at reunions helps us to relive those days. The sound of a whippoorwill returns me to nights on the farm. The sound of someone's voice might make us feel small because it has a tone quality similar to grandfathers.

Sight is also a strong conveyor. When I focus on a blue Christmas light, I get the feeling I'm back at my "childhood" Christmas. Visual regression constantly occurs. One day as I was driving along, the sight of the color of the car next to me caused me to feel regressed. I couldn't readily establish the time, but shortly afterwards I felt as I had when I got my first car. The car I had seen was the same color and shade. Once, during a session, I was distracted by feelings, which reminded me of being around 10 years old. I realized, finally, that the dress my client was wearing was the same exact color of blue as my Cub Scout uniform.

Touch is one of the subtlest senses of regression. The swaddled comfort of being immersed in a warm bath, the pulsing, softly muscular body of a tightly held puppy, someone's special hug, can all return us to an earlier age. Because nearly any place on your body can have a history of various sensations, there must be thousands of possibilities. In fact, opportunities for regression by any one of the five senses would be beyond the capacity to count.

**Regression is Subtle**

Because our five senses are always working, we constantly regress to various early experiences. All is well unless we get zapped with an unexpected feeling. Then the real subtle signals can hit without our realizing what is happening.

For example, you may be walking down the hallway at work when you overhear a man griping someone out over the phone. The tone of his voice matches that of your father or your coach, or your teacher at a time when you were very vulnerable, etc. And, suddenly without knowing why, you feel intimidated. You are confused. By the time you reach your office, you are frightened and shaking. Eventually you have to go home, but worst of all you can't seem to pull yourself out of it.

You call your doctor and he gives you a prescription for anxiety or you smoke a pack of cigarettes in two hours or have several drinks. But actually, there is nothing seriously wrong with you. You're regressed and scared because you've lost touch with your inner parents. Without that feeling of reassurance from your inner parents, you return to the same frightening experiences that occurred when you were a child.

Unexplained regression can be very crippling. People suffer because they may be 5 years old, then 10 years old, then 2, or 8, when actually they need to be 20, 30, 40, or 60 in order to handle their present reality. Self-parenting allows us to take control of the regressions that are a part of everyday life for all of us.

## We May Relive Good or Bad experiences

Depending on the nature of the stimulus, we may relive good or bad experiences. Generally, we try to recreate good memories and abandon bad ones. We will be drawn to fifties' music if we were happy then, but avoid a movie about Vietnam if we were there and had traumatic experiences. Obviously, reliving good experiences may bring us pleasure; similarly, reliving the bad ones can be very disturbing.

A client named Sally became extremely frightened, to the point of near panic, while watching a movie which contained scenes of people killing people. She turned pale and reacted like a terrified little child. Sally said she realized that she regressed to being a little girl who lived in constant fear that her alcoholic father would kill her. In the past, whenever he got drunk, he would get knives or a gun and threaten to kill his children. As a child, she often expected not to live until the next day. As an adult, she continued to live without the expectation that she would remain alive each coming day. After working in therapy on the issue of never again having to face her father's threats, she was able to see another movie showing violence and killing, without experiencing any extreme reaction.

The degree of control we need is based on the severity of our past experiences. When a battered child reaches adulthood, nearly any regression will be extreme and, therefore, a problem. Sally's life was out of control. She had been a battered child and she stayed regressed in a childish emotional state. Now that she has learned how to manage her everyday emotional condition, two important things have resulted. She "defused" the terror-filled regressions to her battered childhood, and began to create good and happy feelings about today's experiences, upon which she can draw.

Some of my clients never face severe problems with regressed feelings from the past. Although their parents were gentle loving people they, nevertheless, did not have the skills to teach them how to handle some of the heavy issues of life. These patients still relive early unpleasant experiences, but are not traumatized by them. If they feel early pain, it is only for a moment, and then it is gone.

Regression is experienced by all of us, and does vary by degrees in intensity and duration. Some clients may work for weeks on one experience that happened to them when they were 6 years old. Others cannot pinpoint a time and age, and may be unable to identify exactly what happened.

The important thing is to come through the experience and feel OK.

## You May Regress to Any Age

Depending on what triggers the memory, at different times we may recall different feelings from any age. We can relive a feeling from an event, which occurred when we were 18 years old or 18 months old. In fact, when preverbal regression does occur, it is difficult to detect. For example, we may re-experience a feeling of abandonment because, at 10 months old, we were left alone for a long period of time.

If by exploring a feeling we become aware that its origin is in infancy, we must allow ourselves to re-feel the full impact of that original feeling, under the nurturing care of our inner mother and father.

I help people, intentionally, to regress to various ages in order that they may return to an experience from their past. It often begins by having them relive a recent experience that was charged with feelings. By encouraging them to expand these feelings into an extreme expression, they are usually moved right back to an early experience.

For example, Charles had recently been with someone he cared for very much. In her absence he was feeling the pain of not being loved and nurtured. I had him call to the person, over and over and over, "Joan, Joan, I miss you." As he did so repetitively, deep emotions began to become evident. I asked him to be aware of his pain, of where he was, of whom he missed as he continued his "emotional mantra".

Soon he was crying, "Mother! Mother! Please love me!" His voice sounded like the voice of a little boy. He had regressed to being four years old, therefore he discovered a significant basis for his feelings of not being loved or cared for. He was then able to create inside himself the love and nurturing that the four-year old Charlie within him needed. And, by satisfying that need for him, Joan's love became icing on the cake rather than a missing basic ingredient.

Sally's abusive husband constantly put her down by telling her how stupid she was. Sometimes his actions became violent. Her response to his behavior was to become very quiet - even to apologize for upsetting him. Sally was barely aware of her anger toward him, but she could certainly feel her fear. In a regression therapy group, I had her relive a time when her husband got angry, tore up something very valuable to her, and broke other things in a fit of rage. By doing this she was able to recall her feelings of fear. Through her confidence in the protective fellowship of the group, she allowed herself to become very frightened. In her fear, she was able to say, "Daddy's going to kill me!"

For the first time in her adult life, Sally was reliving a time as a small child, when her father was drunk and threatening to kill her. Shrieking in fear, she crawled to the corner of my office and curled up in the fetal position, shaking. When I approached her, she said, "Shh, be quiet!"

She was reliving the childhood experience of hiding in a closet hoping Daddy would not find and kill her. Sometimes Sally would regress to being very young, 4 or 5 years old, and at other times she would be eleven or twelve years old. Each age returned her to a different experience which she was able to work on.

Sally was then able to affirm that she had done nothing to deserve her father's drunken rage and abuse - that she had in fact been a good and lovable child. Next she assured the scared, lovable "little Sally" within her that her good, nurturing sober inner father would love and protect her from now on.

After several such sessions of reassuring, nurturing, and loving "little" Sally, she began to make the connection between then and now. She began to tell her husband she would not tolerate his words or his actions. And because his behavior no longer caused her to react like a scared little girl, the confident adult whom her husband now faced stopped his abusive behavior.

## The Regressed Child Often is Confused About the Truth

People used to believe the world was flat because it felt like it. They believed the sun rose and set because it felt like it. This distortion of feeling was not easily corrected even when the truth was finally revealed. When we regress, what felt true to us as a child suddenly feels true to us again. We need a mama and daddy. There are monsters in the world and maybe a handsome prince or brave warrior will rescue us.

I had an English teacher in college who said that when she went to visit her parents for holidays, her grammar and pronunciation went to pot. With all her training; she could not resist regressing to an earlier age before she was educated in proper English. What felt right to her as a child suddenly felt right again even though she knew better. Her parents' home and the holiday setting triggered a strong regression back to her childhood, which she as an adult had not yet learned to manage.

Kay was fifteen years old and wanted to die. She cut her wrists but survived and was brought to me by her father for therapy.

"I just want to die!" she kept repeating. "What is so bad that you want to die?"... "I Am." she said.

Kay was beautiful, intelligent and talented. She made good grades, was a cheerleader and obviously very popular with her peers. But to herself, Kay was no good. Her parents and friends tried to convince her she was perfectly fine but she refuted them all because she did not "feel" OK.

I asked Kay if the world "felt" flat or round and she said flat. A feeling can be dead wrong but still "feel" absolutely true. Somehow in her interpretation of some very early events in her life, she felt that the negative treatment she was receiving was happening because something was wrong with her! She must be bad. If the people around her were so unhappy with her, then she needed to die in order for them to be happy again. That feeling had been with Kay most of her life, but now she was in such pain that she wanted relief. Cutting her wrists was a cry for help and at the same time an effort to get relief.

Emotions based on false information feel absolutely real. When Kay's feeling of being "no good" first occurred at three years old, there was no adult involved in helping to interpret these feelings to "little Kay". Therefore, she was on her own using the undeveloped reasoning ability of a three-year-old. Once the three-year-old approach to problem solving had been instilled in Kay's mind, it took firm root and grew and grew until a change occurred and the truth could finally break through.

Self-parenting is more than just informing our inner child what is true or real. Our child is preconditioned to react emotionally to various situations, regardless of what we, as adults, know to be true. Feelings happen quicker than thought. The five senses are open to receive their signals, and feelings occur in less than a second. Afterward we start thinking about what is actually happening.

Recently I drove through an intersection on a green light. The man in the car coming toward me attempted to turn left in front of me. I didn't slow down because I had the right of way. However, as we passed each other, he pointed to the light and shook his fist at me. Obviously, he thought he had the right of way. He was wrong. Nevertheless, even though I was totally in the right, my heart began to race. I felt intimidated, not because I was wrong, but because I was preconditioned to react to an angry expression. My immediate reaction to this feeling was disappointment that "little Larry" believed him instead of me. But that was not the case. Little Larry couldn't help his reaction no matter what the truth was. So I apologized to my feeling child and began to reassure him that I would take care of him and that the man could not hurt him. My heart slowed down, I relaxed, and everything was fine.

If you believe yourself to be right, but your feelings tell you otherwise, don't get too upset with yourself or let someone intimidate you. Protect your child and hold your position. Then with extreme patience, repeatedly reinforce what you believe to be the truth. Take time every day to restate your truth to your child until your child feels that truth.

## The Capacity to Handle Feelings From the Past Will Vary

When 62-year-old Chloe first came to see me, she was behaving like a child, speaking uncontrollably, imagining things, and was extremely frightened. A chronically critical man at work had harshly criticized her work to her superiors. Her inner parents could not handle the responsibility of keeping the facts clear (Fact: she was not a bad person. Fact: she was not going to be harmed if she were falsely accused. Fact: sometimes adults are falsely accused and still manage). Nor did her inner parents give "little Chloe" the nurturing support she needed. There was no voice saying to her, "I will hold you, I will take your hand and lead you through this situation." She felt like an abandoned child.

After six weeks of teaching her how to call her inner parents to action, Chloe could accept the facts and feel nurtured by her inner parents. Her fear went away.

Nearly all mental and emotional problems are caused by an inability to handle regression. Children or our child-based feelings, cannot deal with the demands of this world, all alone. When we face a problem, which seems insurmountable, there's a good chance that we will become frightened in our feelings and passive in our behavior. In our childish state, we feel our only hope is for an outside source to take charge and save us. Because of our inability to make necessary decisions, we feel confused and lost.

At this point, we often seek unreal ways of coping. Using drugs, becoming obsessed with work or religion, clinging to friends and relatives, or isolating ourselves. Generally, whatever method is used as protection takes us deeper into regression. The only solution is to accept our condition as regressed, and believe that in spite of our feelings we do have the capacity to take care of ourselves. The main function of a therapist is to help us facilitate contact with our own ability to handle life and to get us into action. Help may be necessary from others but wellness can only occur when we accept full responsibility for ourselves. The only parenting needed is available through our inner parents.

For the average person, regression occurs repeatedly. If we treat our child feelings with nurturing care, the consequence is quite different than it would be if we treat our child feelings with the same abuse we received from others, as a child. Obviously, a person's capacity to handle feelings from the past will vary. But everyone's capacity to handle feelings from the past can be markedly improved.

One problem with regression to early trauma is that a person will tend to duplicate the way he was treated as a child. Mary responds to feeling scared with, "It's stupid to feel this way. I don't know what's wrong with me."

When Mary was a small child and told her dad she was scared, he said, "That's stupid to feel that way. There must be something wrong with you."

When John makes a mistake, he says to himself, "You can never do anything right." When John was a little boy and made a mistake, his mother would say, "John, you never do anything right."

Some people bring physical harm to themselves because their parents whipped them severely when they did not obey. Some accidents are not accidents, but deliberate acts of self-punishment. Several years ago, when my secretary was working at Baylor Hospital, they brought a young couple into the emergency room who had poured scalding water on themselves as punishment because they had had sex.

Abusive self-parenting is no different from being an abusive parent. It is a crime against a person. Most self-abuse is of a milder sort. It is common to hear people put themselves down on the golf course. A friend and I were playing golf recently. When he made a bad shot, he laughed first, and then said, "Joe, you clumsy idiot." "I liked it when you laughed, Joe," I said, "but then you were mean to yourself." For my free counseling he offered me a free lesson in golf, suggesting what I might do with the three wood! Actually, he was not offended by my comment because he realized what he did to himself was a thoughtless habit.

If you say talking to yourself like that means nothing, I suggest you ask a small child who messed up how he feels about being called "a clumsy idiot." The little child inside you is equally sensitive. Bad parenting, which started when we were children, needs to stop when we get to be adults and have the power to change it.

People who maintain their emotions with loving care were taught to do so by their parents, or learned how as adults. Some people get angry when they hurt themselves. When I hurt myself, I treat myself the way my mother did. In a tender, loving way, I take care of the injury.

Therapy is primarily for teaching someone how to be a good parent to his/her regressed child-based feelings. Learning to identify things, which cause you to regress, can be extremely helpful.

## II - It Can Be Important to Return to the Feelings of Your Childhood

### If You Were To Adopt A Child

Since I emphasize being good mothers and daddies to ourselves, you may wonder why I suggest we purposely return back to past painful experiences. If you were to adopt a child, two things would be important: First, you would want to get fully acquainted with the child. Learn about the times the child was whipped for no real reason. Learn the awful names the child was called. Learn as much as possible about the child's life experience. The more you can know about that child the better.

Second, you would want the child to become free of the negative feelings that may be troubling him from the past. When the child feels like screaming out of fear but instead remains silent, that un-screamed feeling remains locked inside. In order to feel safe enough to finally release that feeling, the inner parents need to provide the child with a sense of nurturing protection and permission. To accomplish that atmosphere of safety, the inner parents are now willing to take whatever time is necessary to hold and encourage the child. While the child cries about things that happened to him, he is assured that his inner parents are now grown up and well able to protect him from such future occurrences and offer him more freedom to release his feelings as they occur.

To develop the kind of confidence that this builds between the child and his inner parents, there must be willingness to both know and then to release every fear of the inner child.

## Getting Better Acquainted With the Inner Child

Sometimes a new client will say, "I don't know who I am!" What they have done is close off a memory of their painful past. Forgetting painful experiences may have been helpful for survival at that time, but such childhood denial works against us as adults. We need to remember all our childhood experiences, not so we can continue to hurt, but so we can better know and appreciate ourselves. We relive these experiences so we can better understand how the resultant feeling within our inner child is affecting our current life and relationships and so that we can complete the feeling process that has been locked up inside.

Jane had a problem relating to men. She put

men on a pedestal and felt a constant need to please them. In regression therapy, she relived the intense pain of her father's disappearance. She screamed and cried for her daddy. She started crawling across the floor seeking to find him. She was crying out, like a little girl.

Afterward, she was utterly amazed. She said she did not remember much emotional reaction at the time he died. But she had looked for him in other men all her life. Getting to know the pain of the little girl of her past dramatically changed the way she related to men. After she both recognized and released the pain of "little Jane", she began relating to men as an adult rather than as a child.

Shirley would become frightened when she attempted to have sex with her husband. (She had no memory of having been molested when she was three years old.) In therapy she told how she got so scared she would run into the bathroom and lock the door. I asked how she felt. "Terrified" she said, "like I was going to scream." "Be there now, Shirley." She began to tremble with fear. "Shirley, it's OK to scream." I said. So she began to scream over and over again. The piercing bursts of her screams hurt my ears. She became a terrified child. Then she got very quiet. "Shirley, what's happening now?" I asked. "He's coming toward me."

Then she relived, moment by moment the

horrible experience of being molested by her mother's boyfriend who was in charge of taking care of her while her mother went to the store. Later, her mother confirmed what had happened but told Shirley, "I didn't think you would remember." Shirley was no longer afraid of sex after her inner mother and daddy assured her she was safe now.

What you don't know will hurt you. I have had clients who would report the awful treatment they were getting from their spouses. When I could get them to bring their spouses to the office, I too, would find them very offensive. But when I got to know them and the pain they held inside them, I better understood. Not knowing their inner child or their childhood experiences meant I really did not know them. What I did not know hurt my relationship with them, and what they could not remember about their past hurt their relationship with themselves and others.

A couple I once counseled in marriage therapy got into major conflict and separated. They were hesitant to come back to see me because if the marriage therapy we had done hadn't worked before, why should it now? But, they did come back and I reminded them that earlier they had resisted individual therapy and opted for marriage therapy only. Both of them still needed to get acquainted with their own painful inner child's past. This time each agreed to really explore in depth the pain of their past childhoods. Previously, they had neither acknowledged their own pain nor had they recognized the pain in the other. In three to four weeks, they were back together in a very different way. Each verbalized the pain of his regressed child to the other, and that intimacy and trust had the effect of deepening their appreciation for one another.

Just as a social worker must inform a foster parent about the condition and treatment a child has had in order for that foster parent to render the best parenting, so must we know the pain of our past in order to self parent our inner child.

## Releasing Trapped Feelings From Childhood

When a child is being abused he generally remains silent when, in fact, he wants to cry out or scream. This leaves the real feelings trapped inside. If the trauma is not relived, and the scream not released, the pain of this abuse will remain inside for the rest of his life.

Shutting off feelings inside becomes like closing off rooms in the house when they become cluttered with more things than we care to sort through. As each room is locked and closed off we become limited to the available space left to use. Living in one room of a thirty-room house places a serious limitation on one's freedom to enjoy the entire house. I shared this metaphor recently with a client who responded by telling me that she had literally had three rooms in her home filled with clutter and she never used them.

In a documentary, veterans from World War II returned to a battlefield in Germany where they were asked by Bill Moyers to tell about what happened in 1944.
As one veteran spoke, he began to cry. He told how his 21-year-old friend had been shot right next to him. He paused for a moment then said, "I'm more emotional now than I was when he died. But then we were in the middle of battle."
Regression therapy is designed to take a person back to the "scene of the battle" in order to release emotions that have been held inside. Emotions held inside block the entire emotional system.

Such was the case with Ebenezer Scrooge in Charles Dickens', A Christmas Carol. The spirit of Christmas past took Ebenezer back into his painful past in order to release him from the bondage of feelings he had never dealt with. As Scrooge pleaded with the spirit that the scenes were too painful for him to revisit, the spirit reminded him that it was for his own good. Only when Scrooge let himself feel his true feelings about his past was he free to handle the reality of the present and the potential of the future. The result was not only that Scrooge got the Christmas Spirit, but that he got himself back with the freedom to feel all his feelings.

Each week I have groups who meet for the sole purpose of reliving painful childhood experiences. Some curl up in the corner of the room and cry. Others scream in terror and some cry out for their mothers or fathers. Some grieve over a pet run over by a car; others recall the terrifying experience of being molested.

If the pain of these experiences had faded away with time, there would be no way they could continue to relive the experiences today. As long as the pain is still inside, it blocks their full and open experience of some aspects of today's life. They feel little or no joy; they stay confused; they can't share their feelings; they can't experience feeling loved; they can't feel love for someone else. Avoiding inner pain causes reality to be distorted! The avoidance of our painful feelings is the cause of most emotional problems.

By re-experiencing the painful abuse inflicted by her father, Betty could finally acknowledge her own OK'ness. As a child she had defended her father's behavior by blaming herself. Though reality said that her father had problems, Betty defended his OK'ness because of her desire and need for an OK father. If she then had acknowledged that her father's abusive behavior had been his own problem, in a sense she would have had to give him up. So rather than acknowledge and relive the pain of his abusive behavior, she blamed herself for the way he treated her. In therapy, she allowed herself to feel her anger and pain at his abuses, which in turn freed her to be OK. As a healthy adult, she no longer needs her father. She can now be her own father.

Re-experiencing childhood pain is not a meaningless opportunity for self-pity or self-abuse. It is not just hurting without purpose. Its ultimate result is freedom from pain. Our regressed child is now accompanied by our inner parents who promise to protect him from future abuse. It is a process of returning our inner child, alive and well into today's world.

When our early child-self faces a painful experience, it is vital that our inner parent intervene. Basically, we go back to the events and protectively hover over our child. When our childhood mother is verbally abusive, we intervene and say, "That woman doesn't understand. What she said is wrong. You are not a bad little girl!" If our child has been molested by her father, we speak to our regressed child and say, "You have done nothing wrong. That man has serious problems! What he did is very wrong. It should not have happened to you!"

A client, regressed to the age of five years old, and experienced feelings of shame because his mother walked into the bedroom where he was sitting in a little chair playing with his penis. "That's dirty," she said. "Stop doing that!"

I had him imagine himself, as the adult he is now, being in the room with his little boy and saying to him, "You are not dirty. You are just fine. You are only doing what little boys do."

Another client remembers with great sadness a time when her mother left her in the back yard of her home and went to visit a neighbor. I asked her to imagine the little preschooler standing at the fence crying. Then I had her, at the age she is now, hold her little girl-self's hand and tell her she would be OK because she would not leave her alone to feel abandoned.

Sharon's father was an abusive alcoholic who made her childhood miserable. She met and married a guy in high school who had the personality of her father, even though he was not a heavy drinker. During a recent breakthrough in her therapy, as she re-experienced the pain of her childhood, she made a commitment to little Sharon that she would no longer have to suffer the kind of abusiveness she had been suffering all her life. When Sharon refused to accept the continuing verbal putdowns and abusiveness from her husband, he left her.

At first, it was a real struggle because Sharon had such a strong dependency on him. Gradually, though, she developed more and more inner strength. Finally she achieved complete liberation from him. One night recently, she was home alone and she decided to look through her old high school annual. For the first time, Sharon noticed that she was not smiling in any of the photographs. She saw her young face as hollow and empty. Her eyes were fixed in a cold stare. She said she read comments her friends had written in the book. Most of the comments were appeals for a better life for her. When she realized that finally at 39 years of age she had found herself and her freedom, she began to laugh. She imagined she was throwing her little girl up into the air and catching her as they laughed together. What a celebration!

M Tatum

# Chapter 4: SELF-MOTHERING: THE ULTIMATE SECURITY

Sunday was a wintry cold day, but good or bad weather, it was the day we went visiting Grandma and Grandpa at their house in the country. Dad drove his pickup and we all crowded in the cab, as best we could. My brother sat by the door, mother scrunched in the middle, and I sat on Mother's lap. She laughed because I would relax and become a 'lump', not even trying to sit up straight. After all, it was Mother's lap, wasn't it? Where else does a little boy feel more secure?

It was the most comforting place I'd ever known, right close to the scene of my creation. The rhythm of her heart felt, oh, so familiar against my body. The vibrations of her voice resonated through my being once more. For months, her body had been my ultimate protection; no wonder I felt secure on her lap. I felt I belonged there. Mother's lap was warm, safe, and comfortable; the ultimate security.

The day came when I had grown too big. I felt embarrassed to think I had ever sat on my Mother's lap. After all, I was becoming a man and was no sissy! But within my newfound macho exterior, a little boy crouched shivering in the back of the pickup longing to return to the cab, to be warm and safe on Mom's lap.

With the days of Mother's lap gone forever, should the feelings be gone, too? After all, no lap is now big enough, and the idea is ludicrous at best. But feeling warm, safe, comfortable and secure is not ludicrous, and the desire must not be gone forever. Some of us still look outside ourselves, seeking satisfaction of those feelings from others. But the outcome of this outer search has potential pitfalls and very limited possibilities. (Ultimate security can come only from within ourselves.) It is the mother within our own soul who can take us on her lap anytime we want or need her to.

## I - Learning The Skill Of Self-Mothering

Just as the need to be mothered is in each of us, so is the capacity to mother. Men and women both have the same potential for mothering but self-mothering does not come naturally. It has to be learned. We learn it by example from others, through instruction by others, or we teach it to ourselves. Regardless of how the act of self-mothering is acquired, it is an essential to healthy adult living.

Self-mothering provides the way to maturity and, therefore, to security. Making our own selves feel warm, safe, comfortable and cared for is the natural result of saying, "Please, Mom, let me do it myself." Which is, after all, our growing-up response to tying our own shoes or combing our own hair. In the same way, learning to comfort ourselves in our fears should also develop naturally, during the early years of our lives. If we continue to look to outside sources for complete comfort and protection we have not yet learned to tie our own emotional shoes.

The extreme consequence of not being able to care for our own feelings will likely be a very limited ability to function. An individual in this condition must sometimes be hospitalized. On the other hand a mature, autonomous, self-confident individual is one who has mastered the art of self-mothering.

In the book Nobody's Child, both behavior extremes are seen in the same person. Marlo Thomas appears in the TV version, as a woman who has made the successful transition from helpless child to functional adult. As a child, she was not given the care and comfort of effective parenting and she grew up unable to care for herself. The movie, based on a true story, told of this mentally ill woman who was considered incurable and confined to the secured ward of a hospital. A concerned psychiatrist sought the opportunity to work with her and, ultimately, the care, contact, and communication, between nurturing psychiatrist and patient led her to become healthy functioning human being who eventually earned a degree from Harvard University.

In one powerful scene, the woman returns to her apartment after attending the funeral of her husband. Her face is marred with grief. She hears a small voice, the sound of her little girl-within, crying with pain. In recovery she has learned to feel love for herself instead of the severe self-hatred she had felt in the past. Turning around she sees, on the bed, the image of herself as a little girl; she approaches and kneels down to embrace her child-self. Each touches the other's face with feelings of love and deep intimacy, and the scene ends with her lying on the bed holding her little girl. The image of the little girl fades away leaving her folded arms embracing herself. It is a beautiful symbolic picture of self-love - of being her own good mother.

To want and need a mother is a universal condition. Every human being needs mothering. The expressions of mothering, represented by tenderness, warmth, and softness feel good to both child and adult. A mother's care, nurturing, encouragement, and protection are basic to human needs and we never outgrow them.

When a mother provides a good model, mothering will come easier. I remember as a child some of the good ways my mother took care of me. When I became cold and frightened, Mother was there. I ventured too far on my bicycle one day. A north wind blew in and I was so cold I thought my hands would freeze off. The tears on my cheeks felt frozen. I peddled as hard as I could to reach home and ran into the house loudly screaming and crying. Mother put my hands in cool water, then rubbed them until the pain was gone.

When I stepped on a nail, Mother was there to cleanse the wound, medicate and bandage it. I felt very taken care of! When I was sick, she held my head or put a cold wash cloth on my hot forehead. She fed me warm soup and Jell-O. When I took my nap in the summer, she put an oscillating fan on me so I would be cool. In the winter, before I went into a very cold bedroom, she warmed a blanket by the stove. She ran to the bed with me and wrapped me up, then pulled the covers over me. I felt taken care of! When I came home from school hungry, she fed me a snack or gave me a dime so I could ride my bicycle to the store for ice cream.

## II – Taking Care of Ourselves

How she took care of me then, that's how I must take care of me now! Even if she were still living, it would be my responsibility to care for myself today. My body is too big, and I've celebrated too many birthdays, for me to look to any but the parent within to take care of me today. Learning self-mothering began with the way mother parented us. Mother's way of doing things overshadows all other early influences, but regardless of how she parented us, there comes a time when we must do it ourselves!

For me, making the transition from mother's care to self-care occurred only after a great deal of effort. Mother did little to make me assume the responsibility of mothering myself. She never stopped trying to take care of me. For years after I was grown she wanted to wash, iron, and mend my clothes; asked about whether I was eating right, taking my vitamins, had enough money, and was going to Sunday School.

During a Christmas visit she wanted to exchange chairs at the dining table because hers was higher than mine was, even though I was much taller than she was! She meant well, but the outcome made for a "wonderful mother" and a weak child and consequently, a weak adult. I looked to others to mother me and when they didn't, I became hurt and angry. Fortunately, I came to understand that I am the only person responsible to mother me.

Caring for ourselves is the only way to gain the maturity of an adult. The transition from mother's care to self-care (like the moonwalk) is "one giant leap for mankind!" The wanting back on Mother's lap often lingers well into our adult years. When I do regression therapy, I have clients repeat "Mama," "Mama," until they start sobbing. Only a very few fail to cry out for "mama". When they do cry out, the pain of abandonment is often excruciating, because it is impossible for mother to continue to nurture us after we reach adulthood. Only when the mother inside us takes care of the child are we a functioning adult.

Mothers can tell us a thousand times during our childhood to bundle up but over and over we resist and go out in the cold with improper clothing. For many years I hated to go to the trouble of putting on long underwear and sweaters and I would often shiver in the cold, wearing only a light jacket.

A few years ago I decided to take better care of my body and began doing research to find the warmest clothing possible. I purchased the "best" clothing to take the "best" care of me. I finally decided to be a good mother to myself!

I went to a food allergist to learn which foods were not good for my body. I was amazed to learn that some of the foods I ate most frequently were the most harmful. Other foods, which I seldom ate, were the best for me. I started feeding myself better just as a good mother would!

When you love your body, you want to give it the best care possible. A loving mother wants her child's body to be healthy. A mother who severely mistreats her child is a disgrace; likewise when you mistreat your body, you fail as a mother to yourself. Proper nutrients, rest, and exercise are the practical application of self-love.

## Learning Self Care

A caring mother does not allow her child to stay up all hours every night, eat junk food all the time, or vegetate watching TV all day long. She does not neglect her sick child, or allow her child to smoke. Therefore, steps toward good self care:

1. Make a list of everything you're doing *for* and *against* your body.

2. Set up a dialogue method:

    a. Sit in a large chair and place a small chair nearby with a picture of yourself, as a small child, on the chair, or
    b. Hold a doll (self-doll, teddy bear, or any doll) on your lap.
    c. Imagine you have gone back in time to a place you remember as a small child.
    d. Create your own setting.

3. Take the list you made and go over it

item by item. Commit to the child to change anything you are doing to harm his body. Some examples are:

a. "I'm sorry I've been treating you this way."
b. "I want you to know that I love you and will express my love by the good things I do for you."
c. "In the future, I will pay more attention to you and to what you need and want.

4. Learn to be very sensitive to your own needs:

a. Pay attention to pain!
b. Become aware of how different foods and chemicals effect your body.
c. Be considerate of what your child hungers for. Often it is very healthy but if not, be tender when you refuse and give your child another choice until the two of you agree.

5. Pamper the child in you.

a. Whirlpool baths or bubble baths.
b. Self massage.
c. Comfortable chairs and beds.
d. Please the five senses.

**Results:**

1. You will feel better.
2. You will feel cared for.
3. You will develop trust.
4. You will feel loved.

## III – Nurturing is Primary

Of the many things Mom's lap symbolizes, nurturing is primary. When I sold books door to door as a college student, I met a woman I shall never forget. An elderly woman, she was seated in a corner of the room with the blinds pulled. She never came to the door, she just yelled, "Come-on in."

Cautiously, I entered and found a chair. She was gruff and to the point. "What do you want?" "I'm selling books," I told her. Then quickly changed the subject to try to warm her up. I asked about her family.

She snorted, "Yeah, I got kids, but I hate 'em. Kids are like mules, if they ain't workin, they're no good." Her tone changed to a whine as she continued, "They almost never come to see me anymore and when they do, the grandkids are into everything. I finally just tell 'em to get out of my house."

I felt utter dismay that such a mother existed. When I invite you to mother yourself, I mean it in a warm nurturing way. If you were not mothered that way as a child, then you need to rethink the whole idea. Create an inner mother who is tender and life affirming. We all need, want and deserve a mother's warmth.

In an experimental study, two figures were placed in a cage with a baby monkey. One had the shape of a monkey made from hard cold material, and the other was made of a soft warm substance. The baby monkey touched and played with the hard cold figure, but when it became frightened it went immediately to the warm fuzzy likeness of a mother.

The most rugged macho man can be calmed, and sometimes controlled, by a tender, soft, nurturing, loving woman. However, ultimately this need can only be satisfied through self-mothering. How can a man be tender, warm, soft, loving, caring, and nurturing to himself? He can't until he believes he has that capacity within. Some men surprise themselves with the realization that they can be gentle. For example, when a man becomes nurturing to a child of his own he can experience the need to give comfort and care to his injured inner child. The capacity to be nurturing is within every person, as is the need to be nurtured. Once a man accepts this fact, he begins to move toward self-parenting.

Women cry out for "mother", just as much as men. Most of my clients are women. Certainly in my experience, their cry for mother's care and nurturing is as intense as their need for father's approval. In many cases, their need for mother's blessing is even greater.

A few years ago, I mistakenly assumed that women automatically know how to nurture themselves. I thought they needed only to give themselves permission. I became frustrated because my women clients agreed over and over again to "mother" themselves, and were repeatedly unsuccessful in their attempts to do so. Finally, I realized they didn't know how! Women, too, must learn the role of "mother" in self-parenting.

The psychiatrist, Eric Berne, emphasizes the need for a "warm fuzzy" response versus a "cold prickle". Acts of warm kindness, toward oneself, were considered selfish and inappropriate where I grew up. Some churches, in a questionable interpretation of Biblical teachings, emphasize harsh self-sacrifice. The idea of embracing oneself with tender loving care was considered "sinful". Many religious communities still emphasize self-denial and self-sacrifice, while interestingly a healthy self-love enables us to better serve others, as well as to serve ourselves.

Self-anger is a "cold prickle". When a golfer makes a bad shot and wraps his club around a tree, he is really striking-out at himself. It's his fault because he is the one who made the bad shot. When parents use harsh anger to control and motivate their child, it is likely he will treat himself the same way.

Learning to be nurturing toward ourselves is not an easy task. Much of our parental and cultural conditioning emphasizes a negative approach in response to mistakes, and poor motivation. Using self-putdowns to improve our own performance, or to get ourselves to complete a job, is counterproductive. To address ourselves as stupid or lazy seriously discourages our child within. Self-nurturing and self-praise will not spoil our inner child. Approaching ourselves in loving nurturing ways contributes more than anything else does to our happiness and wellbeing.

I don't want to give the impression that nurturing the child-within means the child-within will always cooperate. Parents know there often are times when it is impossible to please a child. Children will cry because they want peas on their plate, so you put peas on their plate and they cry because you put them on the wrong side. You move the peas and they cry because you messed up their plate and the juice has run into their other food. You offer to get a clean plate, but they don't want peas anymore. By this time you're tempted to break the plate over the child's head. Of course, you don't - but you are thoroughly frustrated!

At times, the child-within can be just as difficult. When we feel ill and irritable, nothing tastes or feels good. When things don't appear to be working out, no word of comfort seems to help much. The most important thing to do at such times is offer love, care, and support to our inner child. Do not condemn or reject. To call ourselves names and become disgusted with our uncooperative feelings only makes matters worse!

The rejected or condemned child may deteriorate even more, perhaps separating from us emotionally. When a condition of conflict exists between parent-self and child-self, the two cannot totally separate since they share the same body. In other words, there is no way to get completely away from the irritable child so the best thing the parent-self can do is make peace.

Gwen was abused as a child. She took on the blame for nearly everything that happened, including her father's death, and had little warmth or respect for herself. In trying to get her to be more sympathetic, I asked that she imagine herself as a small child seated in the chair placed before her. I directed that she say, "I love you and I will take good care of you." to the child. Instead she yelled, "I hate you and you ought to be dead!" Unable to arouse, in Gwen, any sympathy or compassion for her child-self, I decided to make her a "self-doll." When I handed Gwen the doll, she handled it like a sack of potatoes. Once she came to the office with the doll under her arm, its head dangling behind her. She even confessed she had tried to tear the doll apart at home.

Eventually, after repeated teaching, she gradually began to get the idea of what to say and how to treat her small child-self. Gwen said she was planning to buy her doll a nice outfit. She also takes care now to see that the doll is warm each night before she goes to bed. The most encouragement came to me not long ago, when I had her embrace herself and she started patting herself gently as if she were holding a small child.

The shared love spread over me in feelings of warmth and joy. "That's the most loving I've ever seen you be toward yourself." I smiled.

**Learning Self-Nurturing**

Nurturing is being warm, gentle, kind and loving toward ourselves. Using harsh self-putdowns, or calling ourselves bad names, is the opposite of nurturing.

Steps toward good self-nurturing are:

1. Seek to recall on paper any time you used harsh words, even in your silent thoughts, to describe yourself.

**Note**: Typical negative expressions toward self may include words such as stupid, idiot, clumsy, lazy, etc. Also, recall times of self-stroking and list acts of warm kindness performed toward you. When you have done this, write in bold letters at the top of the negative list, "LESS". Then write at the top of the positive list (or the invented positive list) "MORE".

2. Set up your dialogue method by placing your doll or teddy bear on your knee. Or, place a picture of you, as a child, in front of yourself. Or, imagine yourself as a child sitting in front of you.

3. Recall to your child the good and bad lists. It's important that you actually speak aloud to the child. Say things like:

   a. "I'm sorry I called you stupid when you forgot to tell your boss about the meeting. I know you are not stupid, in fact, you are very intelligent. In the future, I will refrain from calling you stupid again." (Now imagine the child's response. Let it take full flower in your imagination. It may not be trusting right away, but stick with it that will change with time.)

b. "I'm sorry I referred to you as an uncoordinated idiot on the golf course the other day. Making a bad shot does not make you an "idiot". From now on we will enjoy the game regardless of the shots we make."

c. "I am so pleased at the way you are allowing yourself to make friends and be more open to people."

d. "From now on, if someone is upset with you, I will not join them in their criticism. I will give you full support!"

4. Learn to be more aware of emotional pain and offer support.

5. Notice:

a. If you feel sad.
b. If you feel hurt.
c. If you feel lonely.

6. Physical nurturing is very helpful in these situations for example:

    a. Holding your hands.
    b. Gently stroking your arm.
    c. Touching or rubbing the back of your neck.
    d. Hugging yourself

**Results:**

1. Feel more secure.
2. Have better self-esteem.
3. Relate better socially.

## IV - The Encourager

We have all observed a small child climb on his mother's lap, for just a minute after playing for awhile, then very quickly return to playing. Returning to Mother's lap for encouragement is a vital part of growing up. Venturing out in creative learning ways, only to return for reassurances, characterizes the developmental years of a child. This pattern in some form continues throughout life.

I did a foolish thing the first time I went skiing. After only an hour of instruction, I hopped on the lift and went up to the top of the mountain. I'll never forget that experience. I looked down that mountain and thought, "What have I done!" I snowplowed all the way down because I was so frightened. My legs ached so badly I was to the point of tears. My desire to impress the group turned out to be a crime against myself and, as if that were not enough; I went to the top of the mountain again.

I remembered a little preschool girl crying her eyes out because her parents were forcing her to take skiing lessons. The instructor told her parents they should not force her because she would become discouraged and she might never want to ski. The next year my family and friends went skiing without me. I had become too discouraged.

The following year I decided to use a method of support and encouragement. I assured the scared little Larry that we would stay on the beginner slope for the entire trip, unless he felt confident to go to the next higher slope. Very patiently, I encouraged little Larry, telling him he was doing very well. I reminded him that I would not ask him to go any higher than he was ready to go. I remember saying to him, as we boarded the lift to go to the intermediate slope, "If you look down that mountain and it looks too scary to you, we will take the skis off and walk back down."

That comforted him and he began to rebuild his trust in me as the parent. Before the trip was over, we had worked our way to the top of the mountain, step by-step. One of the trails was three miles back to ski headquarters and I decided to return without my group. Alone on the trail, with only the sound of my skis sliding through the snow and the sight of the beautiful valley below, I felt tremendous courage and a powerful intimacy between me-the-parent and me-the-child. The unity within and the thrill of the beautiful moment created an unforgettable mountaintop experience!

When I get discouraged the little boy in me longs to climb on Mama's lap and lean against her breast and be told what a sweet child I am. I imagine that her gentle hand strokes my brow and my hair and I feel her strength and energy begin to flow through me. She reminds me that I am special to her and, when life becomes difficult, I am to remember that she believes in me. That scene occurs in a split second, and the child is back playing once again. Mother's blessing is powerful - especially powerful now that such mothering comes from within me!

During the development process, the child seeks encouragement from mother and others. When support does not come, a discouraged child may become despondent or even depressed. In adulthood, this child becomes highly dependent on others. The dependent personality needs an encourager like a drug addict needs a fix. In fact, the dependent personality characterizes the substance abuser.

On the other hand the child who receives constant praise from outside parents, can have the same problem. If as a child we are constantly reinforced with words of how wonderful or how great we are, we may never develop our own inner source of encouragement. Healthy approval supports the child with encouraging words and, at the same time, supports the child's own statements of self-praise!

The ability to encourage ourselves is the only sure form of self-motivation. A self-blessing takes only a split second. In a difficult moment, gently stroke your brow or squeeze your upper arm or caress your hand and say to yourself, "I believe in you, you're special to me." Renewed courage will surge within you like a powerful fountain. It's a truly amazing effect.

**Learning Self-Encouragement**

One of the most valuable contributions to building good self-esteem is the ability to sound a voice of encouragement to the discouraged ears of our own feelings.

Make a list of words or phrases that offer encouragement.

**Examples:**

"I believe in you!"
"You are worth the attention I give you."
"It didn't work out but you are not a failure."
"I trust you."
"Hang in there, I'm right beside you."
"You are not expected to do anything beyond your capacity."

> "If you get discouraged, listen to my voice whispering in your ear. You're going to make it you're going to make it!"

1. Memorize the list above.

2. Visualize how your inner parent and inner child will discuss this.

3. Go over each expression on the list with your child.

4. Recall a moment of remembered discouragement in your life.

5. Go over the words you wish you could have heard.

6. Imagine you are another person who has come to give comfort. Speak the words you believe would have helped comfort you at that time. Write them down.

7. Assure the child inside that you will never again let him get that discouraged.

8. Provide external sources of

encouragement and motivation.

9. Determine how to select the right person and learn how to ask for encouragement (Don't ask a negative person for encouragement. It's a sure setup for failure.)

10. Motivate yourself by reminding yourself of how valuable you are! (Don't try to motivate by fear of failure!)

**Results:**

1. You will always be encouraged because your encourager will always be with you.
2. You will avoid depression.
3. You will enjoy the excitement of achievement!

Not long ago I had my heart monitored on a treadmill. I wanted to do well so I exerted my body to capacity. During the last minute when I was near total exhaustion, I kept saying to myself, "You're OK, hang in there, you're going to make it, just a little more, keep on trucking." Even during that state of physical depletion, I felt exhilarated because I was such a good encourager to myself.

## V - Protection Is Essential

One day, when I was in the fifth grade and just returning to school after lunch, two boys started throwing rocks at me. Our house was behind the school and since I felt very afraid that I was going to get hit, my only real protection was to return home and tell my mother so she would make the boys stop. But if I did that, I judged they would call me a "sissy."

I was very upset and the time for a decision was running out. I finally decided that being a "sissy" was less painful than getting hit by rocks, so I went for my mother. She yelled to the boys, "You leave him alone!"

The boys put down their rocks and I returned to school unscathed. I don't remember them ever calling me a sissy, but I do remember how secure I felt walking across the school grounds with mother watching over me. There have been times since then when people have thrown "rocks" at me. Amidst criticism and put-downs, I might have wished for mother to yell, "You leave him alone!" Mother not only nurtures and encourages but she also does a lot of protecting; in fact, if mother did not protect her child, chances are the child would never make it to adulthood.

Since my mother will not protect me now, because I'm too old and she's no longer present, the mother in my soul must protect me. If she does not, I'm destined to hurt. Thank God, today I've learned to be assertive. My inner mom will now speak out. I've heard her say to people, "You leave him alone!" I can now see myself standing on the back steps yelling to those boys, "You leave him alone!"

Recently a client came to me in tears because of her husband's verbal abuse and threats. She told me that as he yelled harsh putdowns, all she could respond with was, "I'm sorry you feel that way," in a gentle soft voice.

I persuaded her to make a commitment to the little girl within that she would protect her and not allow such verbal abuse.

She immediately told her husband of her new

position, and then the test came. Once again he threatened her. She responded, "You will not touch me and I will not allow you to talk to me that way!"

He backed down! She won a victory in the relationship and strengthened the bond between her little girl self and her parent within.

Being assertive is absolutely essential to protecting the inner child. Speaking out on behalf of our child-self is adult behavior. To wait for someone else to defend us can be disastrous. For one thing rescuers may not be available when we need them, and even if they are available, some are so emotionally ill we may need to be rescued from them. The cost can be too great. Our safety and security hinges on our willingness to speak up for ourselves and be assertive.

I once had a dream that helped me to realize my own power to take care of myself. I dreamt about a nurse who was head of training for a group of young nursing students. She was a woman of authority, with a conspicuously large nose and a protruding Adam's apple. She spoke to the girls one evening while they were gathered in one room, sitting around her on the floor. She spoke to them as if they were feeling defeated and assured them she would defend the school against opposition so it could continue. She cared for the girls a lot, and was very convincing. For some reason, I was in the room and related to her as a peer. We then stood and the girls walked out ahead of us as we followed together.

At first the dream was meaningless to me, until I decided to use a method of interpretation, which identified the head nurse as me and - that's as far as I had to go! I began to weep with excitement when I realized a very powerful woman exists inside me, and assures me she is capable of giving me all the protection I need. Since then I have felt more self-assured in my ability to take care of myself.

I saw a book being advertised which purports to offer a black belt in verbal self-defense. If our parents didn't teach us, we must have some source to learn self-defense. Most often, my mother was silent when she should have spoken. As a child, I followed her example.

It is better that we defend ourselves, even if later proven wrong, than to always give in and thus assume we may be wrong. Right and wrong are difficult to define; our courts of law struggle with it daily. If we feel we are being wronged, it may be wise to assume we are being wronged, until it is proven otherwise.

**Learning Self-Protection**

As an adult, our primary protector can be none other than ourselves; therefore, we are safe only when we have learned a viable method of self-protection. Learning to protect ourselves can be achieved through the following activity:

1. Write down all the experiences that you can remember where you were verbally defeated.

2. Decide how your inner parent and your inner child will discuss it. How your inner parent will reassure your child. Picture this discussion.

3. Review each of the scenes and change your response for each. Picture each scene as it originally started, but respond in a strong, appropriate adult way that's sensible and dispassionate. Avoid rebellious, child-like responses that beg further criticism.

**Examples:**

> "Until now, I've listened to your put downs, but I won't tolerate such harsh and inappropriate criticism any more."
>
> "You're talking down to me as if I lack intelligence. I refuse to continue this conversation unless you stop condescending."
>
> "Before I allowed your accusations, but I am not the guilty party and I resent being accused."

4. Assure your child within that in the future you will always speak on his/her behalf.

5. Apologize for having failed your child in the past and ask for forgiveness.

6. Invite trusted friend to role-play a practice session for your "mothering protector". Have one play the role of your mother and another play the role of a person attacking you. Stand or sit behind your mother-protector as she speaks protective words to your accuser. Then change roles until you have played all three roles.

**Results of the above:**

1. You will feel more secure.
2. You will be freer to embark on social experiences.
3. Your new confidence will affect every area of your life.

## VI - Ultimate Approval

Wanting Mom's praise may be a small child's strongest desire. Nothing thrills the heart of a child more than Mother's approval. I think this is especially true for little boys. When I was a little kid I fixed the toaster and my mother was proud of me. My little chest puffed out and a big smile covered my face from ear to ear. Something inside me got fixed and I felt good; all seemed right with the world.

Seeking approval can be a powerful part of adult life, especially with a spouse. I remember a time when my wife was pleased with some task I did and I felt like a proud little boy who had gained Mother's approval. Conversely, just as Mother's disapproval was devastating, so a wife's disapproval can be devastating, unless one shifts to inner approval.

My wife had wanted me to get the intercom radio fixed for some time. On my day off, as she left to go teach school, she said, "Could you check the radio today?" I started to remove it from the wall but decided to check the source of power first. I went to the attic, saw that the transformer was burned out, and fixed it!

I was so excited! Not because I thought I would bask in her loving warmth and approval when she got home, but my inside mother was proud of me! Whatever my wife's reaction might be, I had already taken care of myself. Her praise would only be icing on the cake.

A fifty-year-old client was in tears as he told me that his 87-year old mother had refused to visit him. He was her ninth child, so getting her attention, when he was a little boy, had always been very difficult. Through the years he had tried to impress her so she would notice and show her approval of him. He tried to persuade her to visit him and see how successful he was in business, and what a beautiful home he had. But, she refused. She had always been a stern, business like woman who showed little or no warmth. Nothing would have thrilled him more than to experience a single warm expression of support from her. He figured that since she was 87 years old, this was his last chance. But, she refused him again.

I asked him if he believed she loved him and he said, "Yes." The issue was not about her love. The issue was for him to be blessed with a signal of her approval. However, even if she had come to see him, even if she had acknowledged his successes, he would still feel the need for greater approval. Only his mother-within is able to provide the ever-available warmth, and support to deeply satisfy his grown-up self!

All of our approval seeking must finally be satisfied through unconditional self-approval. A mother cannot follow her child to school, to the playground, to parties, and to sports events to offer constant verbal attention and support. The ultimate blessing must come from the mother within. Even, the most loving mother in the world could not offer enough love to compensate for our own lack of self-love and self-approval. Self-love is experienced only upon our own "laps" as the constant, ever available place of approval.

As children, we were warned not to think too highly of ourselves for fear that we might become too proud. However, in truth it is impossible for us to love ourselves too much! The problem is to "seemingly" love ourselves to the exclusion of all others. But true self-love does not allow that to happen. Self-love is the only sure source of abundant approval, and the truth is that the more we truly love ourselves, the more we are able to love others. Love is a boundless, self-renewing resource, a limitless gift.

**A Mother's Pledge of Loyalty**

> Take your doll, or your imagined child, into your arms and holding close to your body, say, "As your mother, I will take you on my lap when you are weary and discouraged. I will pull you close to my breast and hug you when you are frightened. I will talk with you when you are lonely. I will listen to your needs and respond to you with love. When the going gets tough, I will carry you in my arms. If I need my arms to protect you, I will carry you on my back. During good times1 we will take hands and we will dance. I may not always play when you want me to, because I'll be working to provide you with a playground; a safe place for you to play. I want you to know that I love you

with all my heart, and there is nothing you can or will ever do to stop my love for you. I will care for you. I will nurture you. I will encourage you. I will protect you. I will totally accept you and we shall live happily ever after, forever more. As I fulfill my pledge to you and as you grow to trust me, so will we come to love others just as fully and completely!"

# CHAPTER 5: FINDING YOUR FATHER

One of my favorite stories tells of a father and son who were walking home along a very rough country road, some years ago, in the hills of northeast Arkansas. The son complained that he was tired. His irritability grew until the father walked to a nearby tree and taking out his knife, cut off a limb, trimmed it into a long pole and handed it to the little boy. "Ride this," he said.

The little boy hopped astride the stick as if he were mounting a horse, and pranced the rest of the way home without complaint. Fathers have a way of making life easier.

Every person wants and needs a father who can handle any challenge life may present. And, such a father is within each of us, either actually or potentially. People who have actualized that inner father are responsible, confident, decisive people who can handle difficult situations and are generally happy. Those who do not father themselves have unfinished business with their biological fathers and lack the positive qualities mentioned above. They need, and seek, a daddy substitute.

Good fathering skills are the same, whether in a

father child relationship or between father-self and inner child. This chapter discusses these skills of fathering.

I once quizzed my father about who cared for me when I was an infant. He said my aunt, and various other women, took care of me because my mother was ill. But, he said, often times I slept with him. He spoke about the time when he was in the yard holding me, and someone came by asking him to go with them to a meeting. He told them "no", because he wanted to stay with me. What he related really surprised me because, as I grew older, he hadn't seemed very nurturing; but the image of him holding me when I was an infant gave me a warm feeling.

## I - Need For A Father's Presence

The idea of being cradled in daddy's arms symbolizes acceptance. To receive daddy's approval is a potent need, which lies deep inside each of us. Stories abound about people wanting and endlessly seeking their father's blessing.

Audrey Hepburn told how her father had left the family when she was six years old. She said the lack of his presence affected the rest of her life.

As an adult, she hunted for and found him because she still needed him. She gave him money during the last years of his life and kept seeking his approval through other men. She said she always lived with the fear men would leave her; just as her father had left.

Actor Gene Hackman said the greatest impact on him as a child came when his father drove by the playground and waved goodbye to him. He did not see his father again until he was an adult and, he said, he never got over that loss.

The notion of a father's accepting embrace touches something deep inside us. That approval is often synonymous with life having purpose, as well as with our feeling of personal value. Without father's approval, we may shape our entire life around the hope of gaining that acceptance, somehow somewhere. I once had a client who had served several prison sentences for various crimes. He told me that he never knew his father. The only thing that he did know about him was that he was in prison. He said he got criminally involved, and into prison, hoping that through prison channels his father might hear about him and be proud of him.

It's very difficult to distinguish between receiving

approval of ourselves as people, and approval of our behavior. Children naturally believe that behavior is the most important part of getting dad's acceptance. Today I believe my father approved of me as a person, but as a child I thought his approval was conditional, determined by my behavior.

Sometimes when I sit at the kitchen table and write, I look out the window into the yard and get a yearning to work in the flowerbeds or pull weeds or trim. I see my car or van at the curb and have the urge to repair or to polish them. Not long ago a great realization hit me; my father, by example and work, approved of physical labor but spent little time in play, or reading or writing. I recall that one of the most outstanding verbal strokes I received, as a child on the farm, was Mother telling me Daddy said I had done a good job picking potatoes up off the ground. I worked hard that day kicking and digging potatoes out of the dirt. Because Daddy was proud of me, I felt proud of myself.

The impression I got when I was little, right or wrong, was that if I did hard physical labor, I would get my father's blessing. Since I hated hard physical labor, I opted to get an education in my chosen field, instead. However, I've always yearned for a farm and tractor, a place where I can have horses and work on cars.

Recently I bought some land and a tractor. I also have an old car on which I work. While these bring me pleasure in themselves, I wonder if knowing that Dad liked and approved of these things may be an added factor.

In the movie, "East of Eden," James Dean played a boy who was being raised by his father. His brother was the one who was consistently given father's blessing, and the James Dean "character" felt driven to compete for approval. His behavior was constantly motivated by doing either what his father approved of, or doing just the opposite. He made a great deal of money, intending to impress his father, but his father became enraged when he realized the money was made through the profits of war. In a very memorable scene, as his father rejects the money, James Dean lets the money fall across his father's chest. He tries, unsuccessfully, to embrace his Dad, then turns and runs away crying in agony.

When a person desperately attempts to get his father's approval, and instead gets rejection, he often will turn against himself and become self-destructive, as if his life has no meaning.

## II - Making The Change To Our Father Within Us

Being father to ourselves requires us to do for our inner child the very thing we yearned for from our biological father. Only then, when we embrace ourselves with love, can we find meaning in life and value in self! Not father, nor any other person, can give us a sense of our own worth and happiness.

John struggled most of his life to find self worth and avoid depression. He worked with a therapist for years and made considerable progress. Shortly before moving to a different state, John began seeing me.

He recently called me and requested help to recover from his regression and depression. I listened to him share his concerns in a slow halting voice. I very much wanted to help him, as did his other therapist, but we were limited since our approval was not the cure for his condition. Only his inner father could calm him. And, his ability to receive this comfort involved risking a leap of faith; i.e., he alone could, with no reason or justification, embrace himself and say, "I give myself to you, my son, and nothing in my past, present, or future will stand between us." I explained that this commitment was a spiritual act of faith, which only he could choose to accomplish. There was a pause, and then he told me this was the most hopeful thing he had heard in years.

Alex Haley, who wrote "Roots", struggled to get his father's approval. His father always talked about Alex's brother who was a lawyer. After years of pleading with his father to read his writings, Haley's father finally said, "I read your book and it was very good." "It doesn't matter any more," Alex replied. He had matured; he realized that he no longer needed his outer father's approval.

We all need father's approval, whether its biological father, stepfather, grandfather, uncle, coach, father in-law, boss, husband, lover, etc. If we mature, we will no longer need any of the outer fathers listed above. We may love and respect them and enjoy their company but we will not need them. To need an outer father is to be emotionally crippled. It means we are operating from a regressed child-like state of unsatisfied need. We are little children trying to survive and function in a world where hardships, anxiety, stress, and insecurity make adult thinking and decision-making essential.

Margaret, over sixty years old, became so manic she could not function at work and needed to be placed on leave of absence. When I began meeting with her five days each week, she was delusional and spoke without ceasing. I had a difficult time getting her to stay quiet long enough to listen to me. She would put a pencil or tissue in her mouth to try to keep from talking.

Margaret was an extremely frightened little girl. Her family, church members and minister called me for help to understand her peculiar behavior. I explained that Margaret's behavior would not appear so peculiar if they thought of her as a tiny child who was very frightened.

Her grandfather died when she was five years old, and her father died when she was seventeen. She had loved both of them very much. Margaret's husband had divorced her some 23 years earlier, and she had been struggling alone those many years to raise her children and make ends meet financially.

A conflict at work became the final blow that caused her to retreat into childhood, crying for daddy. She kept saying that if she had had a good husband (daddy), everything would have been alright. Although beyond her understanding at the time, I told her she had an inner father who was the only man she ever would need! Years earlier when she had been in therapy, she had adopted the therapist as father and now she was adopting me as father, too. My role as therapist, however, was to transfer back to her the fathering responsibility. Again and again I reassured her that she had an inner father capable of making decisions and taking care of her.

At first, she was puzzled by the idea, and confused. As I encouraged her to answer her own questions, to make decisions, and to remember her early painful and unfinished experiences, with the power and support of her inner father, she became less manic. In less than two months time, Margaret overcame her delusional manic state and returned to her job a contented and conscientious worker. That was in 1985 and every year since she calls me on my birthday to say she's still doing well.

Learning to oversee ourselves, as would our concerned dedicated father, is the only way to find peace in a world that requires adult supervision and care. Being able to claim and activate that part of the personality called "adult male father", is required for us to feel secure. Our inner child cannot force our inner father to act in our behalf by doing the right things. Our inner father is the result of an act of faith and will; we must believe that somewhere, somehow we have that capacity.

**The Steps To Self-Fathering**

Whether we are man or woman, the process of "Imaging" is the same for each of us. Imagining our father, as a repetitive activity, allows us to learn how to give our inner child, the reaffirming, supportive behavior we need from the inner parent and, allows us to give ourselves this longed for love and support whenever we feel the need! Although the steps we take to reach our loving inner parent may seem ritualized, nevertheless faith and trust are essential. Whenever our actions must precede our belief in success, an '"act of will" is called for. This act of will, combined with feelings of the heart, characterizes the steps to self-fathering.

1. Ceremonies for approval. (No matter how

simple these may seem, they are worth doing.)

a. Place three chairs in the given area. One is symbolic of your biological dad, the other is symbolic of your inner dad, and the third (preferably a small chair) is symbolic of your inner child. Sit in the child's chair and look at the dad from your youth, your "outer" dad. Ask him to embrace you with approval and love. If his response is favorable, let him; if not favorable you will be OK.

b. Next, look at the chair holding you, the mature, knowledgeable and wise adult. Ask your adult if he will embrace and love you. If for some reason he refuses, say to yourself, "my adult is contaminated by his past teachings." If your inner adult is, indeed, so affected by the past, you may need to seek psychotherapy to "de-contaminate" him. If his response is positive, prepare to enjoy his approval and love.

c. Next, move to the chair and imagine

you are your inner father. Imagine seeing yourself as a small child (old pictures can help with the image if necessary). Allow yourself to say, "You are a precious child and I love you very much." If your child seems to withdraw, then he has not yet learned to trust you. You can repeat this experience until you get a favorable response, or you may need to seek help from a therapist. If your child's response is favorable reach out, take him in your arms and hold him very tight against your chest. Feel him melt into you as the two of you become one. The tenderness and meaning may bring you cleansing tears.

2. Maintain the hug

   a. When you awake each morning, sit on the side of the bed for a minute and tenderly rub your legs and arms, pat your cheek, and give yourself a big hug of self-love and approval. This is a wonderful way to start the day.
   b. Just before going to sleep each night,

wrap your arms around yourself and say to your child, "You're a wonderful child. I love you and love being your Dad."

3. During the day

    a. From time to time during the day, clasp your upper arm with your hand and squeeze. Imagine you are giving words of approval and care for your inner child. This is an example of a very quick "anywhere, anytime" supportive ritual of approval.
    b. When you are faced with a threatening situation, hold your arm or clasp hands; if the situation allows, embrace yourself and say, "You're OK, Son. Dad is in charge. You may go play."

## III – Learning About Life

There were times when Dad took me on his knee and played with me. One of the things he would do is "whisker me". He would rub his rough whiskered face against my tender neck and I would laugh and squeal and try to get away.

I don't remember my Dad ever taking me on his knee and explaining about life; I was left alone to figure out so many things. Parents tend to leave their children to figure out things on their own. As a parent, I seldom sat down with my children and explained what was happening to them and why. If they weren't complaining, I assumed they were working through what was happening and were doing fine, but that's not the way it should be.

For example, a father might take his child on his knee and quietly explain that the playmates who just hurt him are, in fact, capable of hurting him again, and, suggest that although he could likely get hurt many times during his life, he would overcome the pain and be able to forgive his friends and resume play. Explaining people sometimes hurt each other, is explaining a fact of life that may help the child realize feeling hurt is not peculiar to him; in other words, nothing is wrong with him. Also, awareness helps him to be cautious at times preventing hurt in the future. A child must learn to live without the illusion that pain is not a part of life; that people really don't ever hurt each other. To live in this illusion, is to live in unreality.

Such rudimentary and simple lessons taught from father's knee, when taught suitably with the age of the child in mind, will be invaluable for the rest of the child's life.

As a child, there were times when I longed for answers, but did not ask for them. When I was five years old, I remember hearing a crash on a nearby street. I ran through the back yard, through the garden, and a neighbor's yard to get to the street where I saw a large truck turned over and a man lying beside the road covered with blood. I felt sick all over. I walked back through the garden, frightened and confused, but never told anyone. If only someone had talked to me, I would have felt better and been more prepared for the future.

Not long ago, I saw a portion of an old "Leave It To Beaver" show. Beaver's dad had entered his room to ask him some questions and reprimand him for something he should not have done; but his father also took time to explain to Beaver the possible consequences of his behavior. I thought how much I wished my father had been confident enough and taken the time to come to my room and explain things to me. I wish I had taken more time to go to my children's' room and explain more of life to them. Maybe the father's visits to the bedroom in "Leave it to Beaver" or "My Three Sons" were idealistic, but the idea matches a deep need in every child to understand how the world works.

Learning about the kinds of problems we may encounter, and the many possible ways to solve them, is an essential part of parenting a child. Without this information, we remain children all our lives, dependent on someone else to tell us what to do.

Belinda called one day, distraught because she had come upon a situation for which there seemed to be no answer. "There must be at least fifty ways to settle the matter." I said.
"Just tell me one," she asked. I suggested she get a piece of paper and start writing possible solutions; that she be creative and daring but also to call the library, as well as other sources of information. "After your list reaches twenty five, call me back and we'll discuss the problem further." I said. She never called. The next time she came for her regular appointment I asked about her problem. She laughed and said, "What problem?" She had "Daddy'd" herself.

Self-direction is essential to maturity and security.

Finding answers through our own personal research, and making decisions based on that research, is vital to adulthood.

When I was a teaching assistant in the Department of Philosophy of Religion, I was teaching a class one day and one of the students kept challenging me about the necessity of learning the various views and approaches to thought so I asked, "What would you rather have? One bullet or the knowledge and ability to make bullets?" He responded, "I'd rather have one bullet." "When you fire it, there will be no more." I explained. "I don't care, I'll take my chances." he rebelliously replied.

Wanting everything to be given to him causes a person to remain forever a dependent child. Self-daddying calls for an inner daddy, who is willing to learn, investigate experiment and make decisions. Without this commitment, one will always be insecure and dependent upon others.

Joe has a prominent position in city management. He is often frightened because his responsibilities are so overwhelming, and he feels nervous and unsure of himself. When Joe came to me the first time, he was so unnerved that it became necessary for him to leave his work that day. He came to the office shaky, nervous almost to the point of tears. I explained to him about the father inside him who could take care of him very well, so he need not feel desperate for security.

We discussed his inner father. Then I had him imagine that his child-self was in the other chair, and he was to say to that child-self, "Little Joe, I will take care of you. You can go play and think about other things while I handle business." I told him to take hold of his left arm and squeeze it tightly and say, "It's OK, son. I will take care of you."

At his next visit Joe told me, "I've been able to do so much better, but I still don't have the ability to prevent being unnerved at times." I set the scene for Joe to take full charge of his life. I placed an image of his inner father in one chair and, in another chair, placed the image of the father of his youth. Then I placed him in a chair that represented his inner child.

"Imagine that the father of your childhood says something that you no longer believe." I instructed.

"He was very prejudiced toward blacks!" Joe recalled.

Next, I asked Joe to imagine himself in the inner-father chair and to speak as he thinks today. "I no longer believe that blacks are inferior," he said. He looked to the chair in which sat the father of his youth, who had been gone from his life and had for some time been deceased. He began crying. "I can't. I can't do this. I can't go against my father. I would feel I was betraying my father." He cried and cried. Finally, I instructed him to say, "I no longer hold your views. I will no longer honor what you are telling me. I will honor my newfound father-self." Slowly, and with deep anguish he said to the father, "I cannot serve you any longer." I then asked him to look at himself as an adult, as the father he is now, and to say, "You are my new father, I will follow you." "I don't want to," he said. "I don't want to, but I don't have any choice."

"Move over to this other chair and be your new father, Joe." I said. "And from this chair say to yourself, "You have an obstinate child who is afraid and angry because he has to leave his old father. Will you be kind to him and give him patience and understanding until he can build his trust in you?'"

That was the beginning of a newfound

relationship! Having broken the ties with the father of his past, he was finally free to be the nurturing, supportive inner father for his present!

## Take Time To Explain Things

No matter how intelligent or wise you become, it's absolutely essential to explain life on a child's level to your inner child.

1. Set Aside Time to Explain

Just as it is essential for good parents to designate time for, and devote time to, their children, so it is with setting aside time for your inner child. There is no other way to do this. Your inner father does not automatically transfer information to the child without it going through your conscious mind. You must speak the words out loud or "aloud in your head", in clear, concise sentences as if you were talking to a child!

"I know you are scared, but I am here with you."

"I know you are sad, and that's okay. After a time, the sadness will go away."

"I don't blame you for being angry. You need to express it, tell the person you are angry at how you are feeling, but don't call him names and don't break things."

(<u>First</u>, you acknowledge the feeling and then you give direction.)

2. Set Up the Talk

You can plan to go to a specific room or you can talk to your child while driving down the road or walking down a hallway. Constant availability for your inner parent to "talk" with your inner child, is essential; however specially designated places and times are important you should go to a special place at least once a week and set up this scenario:

a. Set up two chairs a small one and a large one.
b. You can imagine your child-self is sitting on your lap.
c. You can take your self-doll or another prop and talk to it.

3. The Nature of the Talk

You can share important information that your own parents never discussed with you as a child. Or, talk about feelings that are overcoming your child-self today. Make a commitment of how you plan to be a better parent to yourself in the future. You can speak words of endearment to your child-self and create a spirit of intimacy.

Taking time to explain truths related to life, to your feeling child-self, will save you a lot of pain and trouble.

4. Daddy Takes You By the Hand

Life is scary for everyone. Anyone who claims to fear nothing has a serious problem! Our fears are reduced when we, somehow, come to feel overseen or taken care of by someone more powerful than we are. The large, strong, maybe even callused hand of our father, holding on to our hand in a crowd, reassures us that we are protected. We then can walk with a confidence we otherwise would not have.

## IV – The Connection

When I was a child, our house was not air-conditioned. My bed was near a window. So, in an effort to get more air, I placed my pillow in the window. I had just about dropped off to sleep one night, when a man walked past my window. Since our house was in the country, it was strange for anyone to come that close to the house. Then the man walked onto the porch. I wasted no time getting to my father's bedroom to tell him. Dad went to the door to check on the situation, but by then the man was going through the woods away from the house. Dad said he was probably drunk; so we all went back to bed feeling comforted. I felt secure because my father was there to protect me.

Now when there is a noise I am the "Dad" who is called on by my wife for protection and comfort. I go to the window or door, or wherever, to check on the sounds and my family feels secure. The daddy-in-me has grown up. But I'm well aware that as I go searching, I symbolically reach out for the hand of my inner child and say to "little" Larry, "Hold on, Son. I'll take care of you."

If we have no inner father whose hand we can

tightly clasp, we may be totally overwhelmed by fear when encountering rejection, abandonment, betrayal, financial stress, death of a friend or relative, news of serious illness, or any other tragedies of life.

Our inner father will not shrink from these realities. He will not declare repeatedly, "I can't believe it!" He will not turn against our feelings of pain and fear with impatience and put-downs. But, he will stand tall and strong, holding tightly to our inner child, providing safety as our child feels all of his feelings.

The day I wrote the preceding paragraphs a friend called to tell me he had cancer of the kidney. He said his surgeon was to remove it the next day. I could sense how intense he was. I knew he sometimes intellectualized to avoid his feelings, so I said, "Let me read to you what I just wrote today."

When I finished reading, "holding tightly to our inner child as our child feels all of his feelings," Matt began to weep very loudly. He had sought to be a strong father by believing the reality of the situation and accepting what must be done, but he had neglected his inner child who was very frightened.

On the other hand, if a person experiences life only as the child and reacts from a point of childish emotion, a very serious circumstance exists. Our ability to make necessary adult decisions is essential for us to feel safe and secure.

When we are not in touch with the inner father, or if our inner father is not developed, we will feel like a lost or abandoned child when faced with crisis.

That lost feeling may cause us to believe that friends, family and even God are out of reach. Genuine inner security must come from one's own inner daddy. From the father within, we are able to love, protect and support ourselves which is the only true pathway to feelings of safety and security.

I have enjoyed teaching people a very simple technique for communicating reassurance from the inner father to the inner child --squeezing one's own upper arm very tightly saying, "I'll take care of you!" - has brought reports of some fantastic results.

One day I was sitting with a client when a very financially crucial phone call came in to me. After

I hung up, my client said, "That must have been a very difficult call."

"Yes, it was, but how did you know?"

"You were squeezing your arm!" he said.

Only then did I realize I was holding tightly to my left arm. We both laughed, for I had been working with him to do that very thing in order to reassure himself.

Not long ago, I called a psychologist friend who had been a client of mine. I was upset with him about something and he knew it, but I was not telling him straightforward. He said, "Larry, why don't you just grab hold of your arm and reassure the kid that it's okay to tell me exactly how you're feeling."

We laughed because I had taught him to secure his child and then speak his true feelings. So I did exactly that and told him how I felt. He received it well and we resolved the problem.

## A Call For Contact

A child wants to be touched when frightened,

so it is vital that when you are afraid, you make comforting physical contact with yourself.

1. Arm Squeeze

One of the simplest methods of contact is to take one hand and squeeze your upper arm. When a small child is afraid and someone he knows and trusts takes him by the arm and gives him a reassuring squeeze, the fear usually goes away.

Clasping your hands together and squeezing tightly can also work.

2. Imagining

Size is very much related to feelings of fear. Generally, when you're afraid, you feel small. If you will imagine yourself as small but also picture yourself as a grown adult father standing large above you holding your arm or hand, you will have a better perspective. Also1 picture the adult in your image as much larger than the person or thing of which you are frightened.

I have used both the above methods with myself, as well as with clients, and both have proven to be very effective.

3. Dad Takes You With Him

My dad was in the cattle business at various times during the years I grew up. He carried a long cane, shorter than a shepherd's staff but similar. He used it to punch the cattle and hogs, to direct them and make them go. I had one of his old canes, which he had cut off so it would be short enough for me. He would take me to the cattle auctions; although I knew little about what was happening and really didn't care to know more, I enjoyed being with my daddy. I got very excited when he told me I could go with him. I remember climbing into the cab of the pickup with my little cane and straw hat; glad I could be with him.

Dad's purpose in going to auction was to buy and sell cattle to make a profit. He would examine the cattle, listen closely to the auctioneer, bid, pay, load the stock, and then take them home. That was his business, not mine. My business was to be with him while he did his business. But by being in his presence, I had the opportunity to observe people and life. I was able to experience and learn.

## V – A Shared Relationship

If we shelter our inner-child-feelings we limit ourselves. We cannot be fully alive if we lock our feelings in a room and go off and leave them. To transact any business without acknowledging the presence of our feelings places a serious limitation on us. However, that does not mean our feelings should run our business. A proper balance of rational thinking-business and inner-child-feelings is vital.

Dad was a hard worker who was determined to provide for his family. Although I had the necessities of life, I also needed companionship with my father. I wanted a father who would hunt and fish and ride horses with me, someone who would talk to me about life. I understood that he never had received that attention from his father, and he was driven by the fear of poverty, but that neither erased nor satisfied my need.

After I became an adult, I became friends with a man with whom I would bow hunt, take float trips down rivers and work on cars. Even though he was only three or four years older than I, he became a father figure. He was a very knowledgeable and skilled outdoorsman and he taught me a great deal about game, and about many other aspects of nature. He also knew a lot about cars and taught me how to work on my car. If I got a good shot at a deer or did something to my car to make it run better, he would get even more excited than I would. Whenever I did well, he praised and encouraged.

When my son grew old enough to go with us, I was excited because he, too, could learn from Tom. But as time went on, because Tom had other commitments, my son and I went hunting and floating without him. At first, I would not go without Tom, but I came to realize that it was time for me to be father to my own son the way I had always wanted to be fathered myself.

Many a child thinks to himself, "I wish my daddy would take me fishing. George's daddy takes him fishing all the time. I wish my daddy would come to see me play football. I saw my friends' daddies were there. I wish my daddy would help me fix things. I had to ask Bill's dad to fix my bicycle." Feeling neglected by our parents can lock us into feeling abandoned and unloved.

While I enjoyed being with my father at his business activities, nevertheless, I wanted to be with him for recreational activities, too. Maybe, you might say, I wanted him to be available and involved with me for play activities.

I once spoke with my father about the way he raised us. I told him, "I realize that you grew up in poverty and were dedicated to working hard to provide for your family. But, I really regret that you didn't take the time to play with us." He validated my feelings by saying, "My son, that is one of my greatest regrets, as well."

To a child, being in the company of daddy can be one of the greatest experiences in the entire world. Having awareness today that you as the "daddy" and you as the "child" are always in the company of each other, can also be an ongoing grand experience!

### The Way To Share Life

When you keep a dialogue going between your inner father and your inner child, you are living a shared life and you will never be alone.

1. Make Plans with Your Inner Child

   It can be exciting for you to discuss with your inner child, plans to do things together. You can talk about going to eat. "What would you like to eat for lunch, son?"

   "I want a hot dog," comes the answer.

   "Well, I don't think that will hold us until dinner. What about chicken salad?" says the loving parent.

   "Yuck, no way!"

   "How about going to a cafeteria? I'll let you pick your dessert."

   "OK, that sounds great."

   **Note**: You can plan trips together. You can plan activities together, etc.

2. Carry Out Plans

Don't promise your inner child something and then not deliver! If circumstances prohibit carrying out a plan, then discuss it with your feeling child and consciously revise the plans. Otherwise, you will become angry with yourself and your inner child may lose trust in your parenting.

3. The Intimacy of Sharing

As you eat, travel, or engage in any activity, keep the inner dialogue going. Recently, in mid-September, I was on a trip in the mountains near Lake Tahoe. Big snowflakes were falling. I pulled over to the side of the road and said, "Let's get out and enjoy being in the snow." With childlike excitement I grabbed my coat and stepped out into the snowfall and let the large flakes land on my face. My child self was delighted. We set the camera on a rock and took our picture (with automatic shutter, of course.)

Take your child self with you wherever you go. Do whatever you can to heighten the awareness and enjoyment of your inner child.

## VI – Dad Takes Charge

George has made great strides with the concept of being a good daddy to himself, but he continues to lack discipline in areas such as paying bills, eating properly and attending to other rather important matters. In a dialogue, which I helped him to establish, between his inner father and inner son, his father-self pleaded with the son to allow him to take charge and be responsible; it was very obvious that the authority was with the child. The father within was waiting for his child to give him permission to be responsible. I told him it would never happen! The burden of authority, power and assertiveness lay with the father, and it is always up to the father to appropriately lay claim to this position.

Have you ever seen a parent under the control of his children in a supermarket or mall? Of course you have, so you know how ridiculous this scene appears! The truth is that the parent is depressed because he feels helpless to deal with the child. The child feels insecure because he has no safe adult to oversee him. Therefore, a person feels depressed and insecure when his inner father refuses to take charge.

Will, a very qualified insurance agent, said he could not conduct business because he felt inadequate. I said, "As a child it is true that you are inadequate to operate your insurance business, but as an adult you are fully qualified." We had spent a great deal of time in the past transferring his work from his inner child to his inner parents, but for some reason he still had no confidence.

I set up a two-chair exercise with Will's inner child and inner parent facing each other. Will's inner child told him he was not a good insurance man; his inner child presumed to know more about insurance than his inner adult parent. Here is a classic case of the "tail wagging the dog"! Because Will's child had been let down so many times in the past by his weak inner parent, his child refused to trust his inner parent, even in an area where the inner parent was highly qualified.

So Will's inner parent spoke, "I realize you are upset with me for my past failures, but you are not qualified to evaluate my ability as an insurance agent. From now on, I will operate without listening to your putdowns about my work. In fact, you need the freedom to play and enjoy being a child without the fear that I am not going to make it in business. So, go on and play while daddy gets his work done."

"How did your inner child react?" I asked, Will.

"He looked relieved!" Will smiled.

When the inner daddy takes charge, the inner child is set free.

Ralph, a computer specialist said he often feared the people with whom he worked. Obviously, he was trying to carry on his work while being his inner child. Even though he was very intelligent, Ralph brought his inner child (his feelings) into his work in a major way. I had him imagine himself at work, as a small child, standing in the presence of the large adult workers. Then I asked, "How do you feel?"

"Frightened." he said.

"Think about your current age and level of knowledge and how you presently look. Imagine that you are there holding little Ralph's hand. How do you feel now?"

He said, "I don't feel afraid anymore."

He told me a week later that the imaging process worked great. When he began to feel frightened, he said he imagined reaching down and taking his inner child by the hand and the fear went away!

The world is so designed that an adult is required to manage events. A child must be protected from the bigger realities of life. Our unprotected inner child will feel insecure and afraid. Daddy must take charge to give the child protection.

I recently took my family camping in the Kiamichi Wilderness of Oklahoma. We own some acreage in the area and in order to get to it we had to leave the main highway and climb two mountain ranges on a dirt and gravel road. Topping the second range, the road turned and headed down the ridge onto an old logging trail. The trail, which ran about a mile to its end, had lots of holes; many of them filled with water.

At trail's end we set up camp in a beautiful setting amidst tall pines and oaks. During the night it began to rain. Although we were dry and comfortable sleeping in the van, my wife woke up worried, "Are we going to be able to get out of here?" she asked.

"Sure, no problem." I replied. She immediately went back to sleep, but I didn't. It was difficult getting there, and now the trail would be worse. Finally, after a bit of fretting I became philosophical, "Oh, well, worrying about it won't help," I thought as I drifted off to sleep.

By daylight, the rain was intermittent, allowing us time for breakfast and a brief walk in the woods. The time finally came to head down the trail of deep muddy holes. I remembered the many mud holes my father had driven through in Arkansas when I was a child. He simply maintained his speed, stayed in the ruts, and never panicked.

And that's just what I did. The kids yelled and screamed with delight as I hit each water hole! All along the father inside me was saying, "Just relax, Larry, do your best and then deal with a bad outcome if it becomes necessary." I was relieved when we made it with no serious difficulty, and thrilled with the inner support I had given myself. When my daughter read this she said "you made it fun and not scary. I remember lots of situations like this."

When I was ten years old, we lived near a train yard. For fun, my pals and I went down to the yards and hopped on the trains, as they started moving. We stayed on as they built up speed, then one by one we would jump off. On one occasion, the train built up so much speed that one of the guys stayed on and was carried to the next town.

A neighbor, Mr. Cox, was a train engineer. He saw us in the train yard, and told my closest friend's father, who also worked for the railroad. Jim's father got us together and said, "I don't ever want to hear of you boys being down at the rail yard again. If I do, you are in serious trouble! What you were doing was very dangerous."

His words struck fear in me!

After that, I felt relieved and protected from harm. The child I was had not the wisdom or discipline to stay away from danger; I needed parental help, and my friend's father came to the rescue.

I had thoughts about writing this book for years, but I never seemed to get around to doing the actual writing. I finally decided to talk to a psychologist friend about it and, while waiting for him to be free, I sat in on his weight loss hypnosis session. Later, while discussing with him the difficulty of getting anything down on paper, I realized that my problems were similar to those faced by a person trying to lose weight. I lacked the (internal parents') discipline to get the actual work done. I loved to dream of having written a book, just as one has dreams of being slender, but without a clear decision to take the necessary actions, accompanied by dedication, devotion and discipline, I was never going to complete anything.

When I finally applied my own concept of self-parenting, I realized that the father in me was not committed to overseeing my homework. I needed to hear my inner voice say, "It's time to turn off the TV, Larry, and get out the tablet and start to work on your book." The voice of authority was silent. Consequently, no work was being done. I had blamed my failure to work on lack of inspiration, fear of critical response, no available time, etc. But the real truth was I had not taken charge, through my forceful inner parent, to see that the task was accomplished. And when I did, it happened!

An undisciplined child is unable to handle this world. There are just too many responsibilities. Our feeling child needs direction and commitment to action, and these come to us only from our inner parent.

**Necessary steps:**

1. Establish who is in charge.

    a. Our child self is in charge when our inner parent fails to learn responsibility or when our inner parent neglects the job. Insecurity, fear and confusion prevail as long as our child self is running the show; therefore, our inner parent must take steps to get back in charge.

    b. First, our inner parent needs to evaluate his training, experience, education and wisdom - as these are necessary to do the job and, if it be inadequate, he must get the necessary "parent" training as quickly as possible.

    c. Our inner parent then needs to set up a dialogue to inform our child self that he (the parent) is in charge. Our child will generally feel skeptical, but hopeful. When our child self is in charge, he will try to get away with things, while blaming the inner parent for letting him.

2. The power of discipline.

   The ability to make decisions, and the act of making decisions (which means carrying them out), is necessary for us to function in the world. We face awesome responsibilities, which small children cannot handle. The strong will, knowledge, and judgment of an adult are needed. Our capacity to succeed as an adult is proven to our inner child as he witnesses repeated examples of our appropriate actions.

# CHAPTER 6: SELF-PARENTING WITH SPECIAL PROBLEMS

A former client, Donna, called to say things weren't going too well, "so I would like to come in to see you." At the beginning of her session, she told me she was feeling some depression and acting very emotional. She mentioned that she was extremely busy with work and family. I pulled an empty chair in front of her and told her to imagine herself as a child sitting there.

"How often do you talk with her?" I asked, motioning toward the imaged little Donna in the chair.

"Like I was saying, I have been very busy," she said.

Ignoring my efforts to get her to notice her little girl, Donna began to tell me about a dream. She said she had a dream about a baby who needed her diaper changed and was hungry. But, Donna said, she did nothing for the baby -which was unlikely and callous behavior on her part. She was very disturbed by her dream.

I paused, hoping she would make the simple

interpretation, then I smiled and looked at the chair in which her little girl-self was sitting.

"You mean---------?" she said.

"Yes." I answered.

Donna began to cry; the neglect of her inner child was painfully obvious. Donna agreed to set aside time each day, during the coming week, to talk to her child-self. At her next session, she was smiling. "This is amazing," she said. "I've had a great week." Donna discovered that we cannot neglect to give special attention to our inner child (feelings) and still hope to function well. However, the positive payoff comes quickly when we give ourselves a regular bit of supportive attention.

Our brain does not communicate automatically from one portion to the other. Information known by our thinking inner parent may not be received by our feeling inner child. For example, our inner parent may feel confidant that he, or she, can take care of our child, but our inner child may still feel insecure. That's because the inner parent has not yet effectively communicated to the inner child, his ability and intention to take good care of him.

Trust develops between our child and parent-selves, when a high level of intimacy occurs in the communication process. Intimacy is essential to inner trust and peace. A husband can hang a sign on the wall that says, "I Love My Wife", but if he never tells her with deep feelings, the relationship remains cold and the trust level is weakened.

Recently, I was feeling continually agitated over financial matters. Finally I imagined "little Larry" sitting across from me in another chair. I told him I had matters under control and would protect and provide for him. His response surprised me. He said, "I know, but I just wanted you to take some time to talk to me about it." Internal displeasure occurs when we don't take time for ourselves.

This chapter is about feeling we do not have the ability to take care of ourselves; not communicating our intentions to take care of ourselves, and the problems that arise. Applying these examples may call for a great deal of personal effort, and even require the help of a therapist.

## <u>I - Problems Related To Specific Feelings</u>

**Anxiety**

Children understand fear; it is one of the earliest identifiable emotions. We start out in this world afraid; especially we have a fear of falling and of loud noises. If we do not develop the ability to distinguish a real threat from what is merely the appearance of a threat, we get into trouble with our feeling system-- we become anxious.

If we overdo our fear of real threats, we live under stress. A few years ago a young woman came to me in grief over the death of her son. He had died in the dentist's chair. She recalled that on the way to the dentist's office, her son was frightened that he might die. She said she told him, "No one dies from going to the dentist."

There are no absolute guarantees in this world, but we cannot stop living fully because of real threats. We cannot stop riding in cars because of wrecks or flying because of crashes or eating for fear of food poisoning. The mother and daddy inside us tell our little child-self not to be afraid, but to enjoy life for the good things it has to offer. Our inner parents also have the good sense not to run unnecessary risks, and to provide us sensible protection.

Betty was afraid to drive her car. She would shake all over with intense fear. I had her picture "little Betty" sitting beside her in the car and suggested that she talk to her. As mother, she was to tell "little Betty" that she was a good driver and that "little Betty" could believe in her to take the best of care. The problem was that Betty was regressing into being the child while she was behind the steering wheel. By doing that, "little Betty" became the one who was in charge of driving the car, the one behind the wheel. And, poor "little Betty" really didn't know how to drive! That's what many of us often do. We turn the steering wheel of our lives over to a child, every time we regress in our feelings.

Feeling forced to complete a task for which we are far too young cause's tremendous fear! The fear of a three year old alone in an elevator, or being among strange people in a flying machine called an airplane is too much. When the regressed child is cut off from the inner parent, anxiety takes over. In Betty's case, she soon learned to take adult responsibility for driving a car and to let her child-self be the passenger. Her fear then went away.

## Exercises For Dealing With Anxiety

1. Acknowledge your true age; this is very important when dealing with fear.

    a. Look at your driver's license in order to view your current picture and see your birth date.
    b. Quickly review, in your mind, the events of your life up to the present in order to become aware that you are not a child.
    c. Look in the mirror and see that you are not a child.
    d. Say to yourself, "I am (full name). I am (years old). I am not a child. I am an adult capable of dealing with the world.

2. Acknowledge the child within you.

    a. Do not condemn yourself for being afraid. That is not the way to help a child.

b. Visualize your child-self as separate from you but very near: in your lap or holding your hand.
c. Assure your child that you are old enough and know enough to take care of him.
d. Practice this process daily. Sounds easy and it really is too! But, the actual doing of such simple little rituals on an everyday basis is not easy for most of us to achieve.

## Guilt

One of the most crippling emotions is guilt. Guilt may help a child stay out of the street or restrain him from taking something which does not belong to him, but a healthy adult knows the danger of traffic and decides not to steal because of chosen values. If an adult feels guilty, it means he is not yet in charge of his own behavior. He has old "psychological tape recordings" still playing his condemning parents' voices in his head.

The ultimate feeling of guilt is the shame of being alive. A child cannot distinguish between himself as a person, and his personal behavior. If his behavior is bad, he thinks, then he must be a bad person who does not deserve to live. When parents do not help a child distinguish between their acceptance of him as a person always, and their rejection of his unacceptable behavior, the child grows up confused. The message, "I love you, but I don't like what you're doing," is essential to good parenting, yet that clarity is often missing for children.

Lois recently took an overdose of sleeping pills; somehow she survived. When asked what went wrong she said she attempted to take her life because she didn't deserve to live. She could never please her mother or grandmother; consequently, she could never please herself. She went to church and served in many capacities including mission trips. She tried to do everything she knew to be good, but never felt good enough. Lois lived a life of guilt and depression.

Our conscience is programmed like a computer. It feeds back what is put into it. If we are condemned as a person, "You're stupid. You're no good. You're too much trouble. What's wrong with you? Can't you ever do anything right?" Our conscience will record these messages and play them back while we are growing up, and will continue throughout adulthood unless our inner mother and father interrupt and correct the messages. Our inner guardian parents must take our inner child into their arms and explain that those old "psychological recordings" in our conscience are wrong. We are valuable, precious people who will continue to make human mistakes. We are not the negative, condemning messages we were given.

Lois told her little girl that she loved her and would protect her from the condemnation of her mother and grandmother. She looked at me and smiled, with an expression of victory in her eyes. At our next session, she brought these words of commitment to her child:

**"Little One... I Love You!**

Little Girl, you are mine now and I will never let you go... nor will I ever let anyone come between us again...

I am you and you are me... Little One... I love you so... Nothing can destroy you now for through me they would have to go... I commit my love, my strength to you... My little one... my love...

At times, I feel the vacuum of darkness trying to enfold me in its emptiness...

That is when I will look at you and say, again... 'Little Girl, I love you so...'

I will take you in my arms and stroke your soft cheek... I will hold you close to me so you may hear my loving heartbeat...

I love you so, my little girl, and I know that you love me... For I am you and you are me...

And together one day We will be..."

Lois told me that, for the first, time Mother's Day has real meaning for her- she now has the mother she always wanted, a mother who will not make her feel guilty. There is a cure for guilt it is when our inner parents stand between old condemning "tapes", and our tender little child!

Guilt originates from old "tapes", recorded with faulty information from parents who may have meant well but nonetheless, told us condemning things about ourselves. The risk of redoing those "tapes" is a feeling of betraying our beloved parents, even though intellectually we believe those tapes are wrong. The messages make us feel guilty, and yet the idea of discarding them also makes us feel guilty - a classic double-bind. Our loving, caring, nurturing, inner parents are called on to "love us out" of the old tapes. If we are loved and cared for by our own inner parents, then the risk of losing the blessing of our childhood parents, by departure from their teachings, is minimized. Often our childhood parents turn out to be glad when we finally drop the old "tapes", which may also have been hell for them to attempt to live by! The "chains of behavior", when finally broken are often, though not always, met with great sighs of relief.

## Exercises To Deal With Guilt

1. Loving your child into freedom from guilt.

a. Hold a prop (use your self-doll or imagine you are holding your inner child). Acknowledge the guilt and tell your child that you are going to help him/her to no longer feel bad about him/herself.
b. Assure your inner child of your unconditional love.
c. Verbalize a commtment to never abandon yourself no matter what.
d. Explain that you will continue to love, protect and care for your inner child, although your behavior may not be perfect.
e. Then tell your inner child you will be responsible to answer any feeling or thought of self-condemnation.

2. Facing the old "psychological tapes" playing messages from your parents.

a. Tell the child you will go with him/her to face the parents, when the tapes start to play.
b. Visualize holding your inner child's hand in the presence of your parents.
c. On behalf of your inner child, tell

your parents that it is you who will now establish the rules.

d. Imagine that you are departing from the scene with your inner child in your arms.

3. Daily maintenance

a. When you awaken, assure your inner child of his/her goodness.
b. When you feel guilty, affirm that you are a person of value, although your behavior has not yet reached perfection - and probably never will.
c. Review those old "psychological tapes" to see what your inner child may be hearing. Example: "Be perfect. Don't ever fail. Don't make stupid decisions."
d. Correct the messages in these "old tapes" with your current understanding. (Since our minds are not like electronic tape players, we are unable to instantly record over our old messages. Much more like a stone-age recording system, the substitution of new understanding for the old requires

steady repetition until the new message eventually "grinds" through and replaces the old tape.)

e. A good sense of humor helps. Laughing at our unreal expectations allows us to put things in proper perspective.

## Depression

Depression incorporates, but goes beyond guilt. It is often described as feeling trapped and cut off, with an overwhelming sense that the really important things - the really good things - in life will never happen for us. Believing that we will be unable to attain these requirements for happiness, we may conclude that life is not worthwhile. Such feelings are based on myths. Belief in these myths, the common lies of life, is entered into when we are children. When regression to a child-state occurs, we return to the depressive feelings we experienced at that time.

If a child is told that by failing a certain task he is no good, then failure will mean depression over being no good as a person. If, for example, a child felt denied mother's love when he disobeyed mother's rules, he will again feel depressed when, as an adult, he breaks one of mother's "rules". And, that will happen whether mother is present, absent, alive, or even deceased. If we feel we must earn happiness and well being by observing all the rules, we will be chronically depressed.

Depression has its roots in childhood. Generally, it's because a child feels required to make one or both parents happy, and the expected way to do that is to be a perfect child. This is a double whammy. First, since perfection is not achievable for any human being, the child's failure is assured. Second, it is impossible for us to make another person happy! If we make that requirement a condition for being OK, we will continually fail and be depressed over "being a failure". Having to achieve the impossible before we can be happy means we will never be happy. Such a child, growing to adulthood, continues to contrive impossible scenarios trying to be happy. She may attempt to make the most unreasonably demanding teachers happy. He may try to make his most cruelly demanding peers happy. He or she may marry an unhappy person hoping to make him happy. The inevitable failure creates depression.

Helping the child, whether still in childhood or within an adult body, to accept his limits provides relief. To permit ourselves to have limits and still be OK as a person, will nullify or erase the depression.

Alice sat facing an empty chair where she imagined her father was seated. She tried to say, "Daddy, I can't make you happy," but choked on the words. She was about to give up a lifetime dream, a dream of receiving her father's approval. Though that "dream" had made a nightmare of her life, how could she turn it loose? The truth, which she had come to believe, encouraged her to continue - to finally say the words, "Daddy, I can't make you happy." Although she felt greatly relieved, another test loomed before her. She imagined her husband sitting in the chair. "John, I can't make you happy. Only you can do that." Somehow those words came easier, because the original contract was with her father. Her depression began to lift. And, with repetitive reinforcement of these newfound truths, depression became a harmless part of Alice's past.

Since depression is a problem of very strong feelings based on longstanding, ingrained untruths, self-parenting requires a lot of patience. Even when we know that the basis of our feeling is a myth, depression does not automatically go away. It is the same as when, having been bitten by a big black dog as a child, we became afraid of dogs - and, even when we "grew up" and knew that a certain dog would not hurt us, it did not keep us from still being afraid. The feeling of depression may be so automatic and immediate that we are overcome before we realize it. Taking slow deliberate steps to reach the depressed inner child is essential.

Degrees of depression have a wide range. A person may be mildly depressed or severely depressed. Extreme depression may require one to be hospitalized. Some forms of depression indicate the need for psychotherapy. If your depression is relatively mild, then the following steps may help.

**Practical steps for overcoming depression:**

1. Acknowledge that you are depressed. Common statements denying depression include:

a. "I'm not getting enough sleep."
b. "Things just don't seen to be working out."
c. "I'm just not motivated- I'm bored."
d. "Everybody's down on me."
e. "I'm just a failure."
f. "Nothing I try helps."

**Note**: All the above statements can end with, "Therefore, I must be depressed."

2. Statements of admission are: I get depressed when I...

a. Try to make others happy.
b. Try to go beyond my limits.
c. Think I need to be someone I'm not.

3. Reassure your inner child of his 'OK-ness" by nurturing the child.

a. "I love you just the way you are."
b. "Let me hold you until you feel better."

**Anger**

Anger is primarily a result of pain. Often

we hurt because we do not adequately protect and provide for our inner child. If we let our child become too needy of others, we hurt and then get angry whenever we feel rejected. If we let people abuse us financially, physically, or verbally we hurt and become angry. Anger, therefore, usually begins within. Our child feels neglected by our inner parents and feels hurt, then strikes back with anger. It is our inner parent's responsibility to use wisdom and assertiveness if required, in caring for our child.

Picture this scene. You are a small child and have gone with your parents to visit a Great Aunt. She is a very generous person and loves children. While in her home, she pays you a lot of attention and periodically asks, "Would you like something to drink? Would you like some candy or some apple pie?"

With each offer, before you can answer for yourself, your parents speak up and say, "She doesn't need anything to drink. She doesn't need anything to eat." Do you remember how irritated you felt at your parents when they behaved in that way?

"How do they know what I want. They must not care for me as much as Auntie does. They never let me talk."

Today as an adult, when you are offered something and you don't at least acknowledge your inner child's wants, that inner child becomes angry at you.

Giving our inner child a cookie, or some other "treat", so he will be quiet and not make his needs known, is a trick we sometimes play. Using the least possible effort in order to placate our inner feelings is a form of expediency ... an attention-giving short cut, which hurts our inner child.

We say to ourselves, "That will do." When we make only a puny effort to provide for our inner child, we are, in effect, offering an emotional snack when the child is entitled to a full meal. We may think we are living a disciplined life when, in fact, we are abusing our inner child.

Expense can be a factor, but providing time for our child need not involve additional expense. I love music. I have owned a

MP3 player for over two years. Finally, I decided to listen to it since, as I mentioned, I love music. Why wait two years? Was I not worth the trouble, for all this time? Did I not have permission? In truth, it was more like, "I'll be OK without bothering with it. After all, it takes time to find the tapes and hook up the equipment."

I wrote the previous three paragraphs in anger! That's because I'm writing from the neglected child's position. If I don't oversee myself, no one else will. Therefore, I'm angry at the kind of thinking which causes me to neglect myself. Just taking care of the minimum and getting by, invites our inner child to become negative. The inevitable result: a person divided against himself.

Providing toys, play opportunities, and time to interact is essential in good parenting. That is just as true for our inner child, as for any other child in our lives.

Some of my angriest clients are those who have severely neglected their inner child. They are mad at the world! A few years ago, I counseled a young man who had taken a stick and beaten in the hood of a woman's Mercedes - because she did something in traffic he didn't like. This young man would drive down the highway with his hand sticking up through the car's sunroof - giving people the finger. He never had learned to parent himself and when he expected the world to take care of him, he was always disappointed.

The world is not going to parent us! It's not supposed to! This young man began to learn that it was he who was responsible for his feelings and his actions. Although his childhood parents continued to provide him with a job, car, housing, clothing, etc. - he was extremely angry at them. Of course he was angry! He was grown man who had never developed his own inner parents, and so was incapable of caring for himself. His anger came from his fears of helplessness.

He gradually began to learn how to provide for himself. He started selecting his own clothes and the type housing he liked. During several sessions all he could talk about was moving to San Francisco.

He had tried once but was not then mature enough to survive on his own. Now he was ready - he had learned to parent himself.

He later called to tell me that he had two jobs, his own apartment and loves living San Francisco. He no longer is angry at the world, or at his childhood parents, because now he is taking care of himself. He is enjoying his self-sufficiency - and the sense of safety he gets from his inner parents.

"Parenting our emotions" means teaching ourselves what to do with our emotions. When we are children, we get angry but do not know what is appropriate to do with that anger, until we are taught. Knowing what it is acceptable to do with anger, or with any other emotion, is not inborn or natural. As untaught children we may break things or turn the anger inward and bite ourselves, or hit our heads against the wall. When we are old enough, we will imitate our parents and /or others. We need to be told to express our anger verbally, by saying what we are angry about. We can be directed to hit something soft like a pillow or bed, or to physically work out our frustrations. If we are told our anger is a normal feeling that needs to be appropriately expressed, we can grow up relating to anger in healthy ways.

If we were not taught how to handle anger, it is important that we teach ourselves. This is very difficult to do, because we must be rational and irrational at the same time. It is hard to think clearly when we are angry; however, it is vital that we stay rational. By getting the rational and the irrational aspects to work together, we can direct our anger in positive ways. We become our own "good parent"; one who stands protectively over his child helping him to direct his anger in good and constructive ways.

Anger toward people and situations needs to be verbalized and acted out in appropriate ways. Also, we must attend to our emotional inner pains and discomfort. If the conflict is between our inner child and our inner parent, no outward change will bring relief. The wall of resentment between child and parent must be resolved. A peaceful cohesive bonding between child and parent will alleviate internal anger.

## Important Steps To Relieve Anger

1. Acknowledge your anger as real. (The worst thing you can say to a child is, "You're not angry or you shouldn't be angry.")

2. Verbalize clearly to yourself the nature of your anger. (This may not be easy because of old "psychological tapes" about anger, i.e., "It's not nice to be angry," etc.)

3. Look for the pain (often fear-induced) that is producing your anger. Arrange to relieve the pain. Verbalize by saying, "I'm angry because I'm hurting so badly. I'm hurting so badly because (example: I feel you are rejecting me because you are ignoring my needs)."

4. The energy which develops from anger may be valuable for asserting yourself in the face of an abusive situation. (i.e., your inner parent's wisdom and your child's explosiveness can be a powerful team so long as you can keep them teamed

together).

5. Unprocessed anger is too costly to your well being. Unload it.

6. Complete your anger and let it go. Enjoy the full benefits of forgiveness.

7. Forgiveness can bring more relief to you than anything else.

## II - Problem Situations

In a moment of crisis, allow yourself the strength of your mature adult and the sobs of your little child. They both go together and, as your team, they can manage any crisis. If you act only as the mature adult, you deny your true feelings. If you are acting only as your sobbing child, the crisis is too overwhelming. People sometimes react at funerals in one extreme or the other. To have a display of emotions is certainly normal and appropriate. In fact, to be only adult isn't normal in a moment of intense grief. Security in crisis comes when your inner feeling (child) is fully acknowledged, and your strength of mind (adult) assumes full responsibility. Security occurs when we make a commitment not to betray ourselves, no matter what happens to us. We agree not to ignore our feelings, not to reprimand our feelings, and to be loving toward our feelings.

### Accidents

> A 31-year old client, named Dottie, recently told about an accident she was involved in when she was 20. She said she slowed down for a stop sign but failed to stop. She hit a teenage girl who was riding a bike. Dottie said that she acted very

responsibly. She stopped her car and went to the aid of the girl, stayed with the girl until emergency help came and then accompanied the girl to the hospital. Dottie gave the police and the hospital personnel the information they needed. Remaining relatively calm and cool until her childhood parents arrived, Dottie said, she then fell apart. She wept and shook and felt like a frightened child. Dottie had been able to inner parent herself very effectively until she saw her childhood parents. With them present, she regressed and became very much a child.

It is extremely important not to regress during an accident. Parental maturity is essential for critical decision making and to reassure your inner child. Panic is another word for being like a frightened child. To abandon your inner child during a crisis, such as an accident, is the same as abandoning any other child when he is in desperate need.

Not only is this true during the time of an accident but also during the recovery. Several years ago, a 15-year-old boy whom I knew, was working for his uncle in a meat processing plant. He lost his arm in a tragic accident. When I went to the hospital to see the boy his mother told me, before I entered the room, that his attitude was good. She told me that when she had tried to open a little bag of sugar for his tea, he took the bag and said, "Mother, I will have to take care of myself someday so I may as well learn to do it now." He took the bag, tore it open with his teeth and dumped the sugar into his tea. He could have waited longer before starting the recovery process, but he wisely realized that self-parenting was inevitable.

Recovery is perhaps the hardest part of any accident. With a commitment to loving yourself, nurturing your pain, being sympathetic with your limitations, recovery is accelerated. The most dreadful scene imaginable is an injured child with an inattentive, unsympathetic parent. On the other hand, loving, caring parents can bring an injured child to what seems a miraculous recovery. The key to handling any crisis is a respectful and loving balance, and bonding between our parent-self and our child-self.

## Stages of Coping With An Accident (Or Similar Crisis)

1. Initially the inner parents have to be in charge, because clear thinking and decisiveness are essential to handling the situation.

2. If your child-self is on the verge of a panic, appeal to him to wait - tell him that you will get to him as quickly as possible.

3. When the danger is gone, hold yourself (your inner child) and allow her to experience her full range of emotions. If you want privacy, seek it, or if necessary demand it - but don't delay any longer than is absolutely necessary, or neglect to respond to the needs of your child-self.

4. You may be faced with parenting yourself through fear, anger, guilt, or possibly depression so be prepared to respond appropriately. For example, a client told me that her very small child had pulled a hot iron off the ironing board and onto himself, when she was in another room. At the hospital, her husband continued to

"gripe her out" for neglecting the child. The doctor stepped in, shook his finger in the man's face and said, "Leave her alone. Don't you understand the word accident?" The doctor interceded in defense of the mother - and her inner child - which she was not able or willing to do for herself.

a. If you feel guilty, forgive yourself immediately. Don't chastise yourself for an accident. Self-criticism serves no positive purpose for your inner child. Any necessary caution, taken in the future, will occur because your wise inner parents have learned from the accident.
b. If you are angry, you may need to express it. If you are not going to express it, get rid of it through forgiveness.
c. If you are frightened, you may need to offer every possible assurance that your inner child is safe now. That he or she will be OK.

**Illness**

I wrote the following while on an airplane:

I'm feeling sick right now and thought I'd

describe what is going on inside me. Currently, I'm in a plane over Arizona en route to California. I have been reading and I am apparently experiencing some motion sickness. My first response is to be emotional. I feel like crying. I am regressed. However, my inner parent has quickly responded, assuring me it really is motion sickness, and a period of time spent looking out the window will help. My inner feelings did not improve until I actually communicated the words inside my head, from the adult to the child. Clear communication is essential to comfort.

We cannot assume that our child will always understand just because we are one and the same person. Words of comfort must be told by the inner parent to the child. I did that a moment ago and now I feel better. I began feeling better only after I heard those words from my inner parent.

Learning to parent ourselves during illness has always been difficult. When we are ill, our bodies lack the strength to support us in the adult parent state, so we regress to our old childish feelings. Many people whine and whimper, like small children, when sick. Without physical strength it is more difficult for our inner parent to feel power. My father, who was blessed with good physical health most of his 85 years, began to weaken a great deal. He was frightened and child-like because his body no longer had the physical strength to take care of him. I asked him to tell his little inner boy, "I will ask for help anytime I need it, and will see to it that you (my child) are well fed and well cared for."

Receiving help from others is one valid and effective way to take care of our inner child. A person who will neither ask for help, nor allow others to help when they are willing, poses a real threat to his inner child. Such a person would rather let his child-self suffer than ask others for help. Therefore, illness creates insecurity through the struggle between pride and dependence.

Accepting our illness as a part of reality allows us to take the necessary steps to care for our child. Grieving our loss of strength, or our ability to feel good, is an important aspect of accepting our illness. But the grief needs to be short lived in order to get on with the acceptance, and the steps necessary to get well.

Visualizing can be very helpful. Picture in your mind being held by yourself, as you would by a loving parent. Imagine the parent telling you how much you are loved and all the caring things that are going to be done for you while you are ill. Children do not want to know technicalities or a philosophy about why they are ill. All that concerns the child is the tender loving care they will receive.

In fact, when illness is not over-analyzed and made morbid, recovery is quicker. Norman Cousins, who "laughed" himself back to health, has testified eloquently to the healing power of laughter. Figuring out ways to get our child to laugh may be the best thing our caring inner parents can do.

## Steps To Parent Your Ill Child

1. Believe your child when he says he is ill. To deny that you feel bad is to neglect your child. (Like the epitaph on the tombstone,

"I told you I was sick.")

2. Offer your concern and care by being attentive to each need of your ailing inner child.

3. Provide some form of entertainment to bring humor to your child, even though you may not feel like it.

4. Nurturing has healing power! Hug your child. Say, "I love you" over and over and over.

5. Be very patient throughout the illness. Never, never get angry at your child! Your child is particularly fragile and sensitive when she is ill.

6. When your child has recovered, celebrate. Plan the festivity ahead of time. Be really creative. It's a fun thing to do so do it thoroughly and well.

## Financial Problems

When I received a bill from the IRS for thousands of dollars, because of a disallowed tax investment deduction, my stomach was flooded with acid and I felt weak. I told my wife about the bill and said I was going to call my lawyer and CPA. It was Sunday so I could not reach either one of them, however, before I called I took hold of my own arm and, squeezing, said to my terrified inner child, "Your dad and mom (my parents within) will take care of this."

When I returned to the room, my wife inquired if I had talked to anyone.

"Yes," I said.

"Who?" she asked.

"Myself, and I feel much better."

When parents talk, in the presence of children, about being unable to pay the rent the child fears he will have no place to live. When they speak of losing their job, the child fears he will have no food. When a parent says, "I don't know how we can make it, "all kinds of terrible fantasies are created in the child. Its OK for a child to know some of the financial concerns of his parents, but children must be reassured that they need not be concerned about lack of food, clothing or a place to live. Children should not be allowed to imagine excessive or inappropriate hardship, as they may likely do without parental reassurance. It is equally important that our inner child receive parental comfort and protection.

When we face financially stressful situations, it is important to avoid creating monsters which do not exist. It is up to our internal parents to dispel unrealistic fantasy. "We will make it," we are reassured. "All our basic needs will be cared for." Fear subsides when our child self trusts our inner parents to take care of the situation. Our trusting inner child does not have to know "how" it's going to be worked out. The answer to "how" is the job of our inner parents.

Anytime we feel fear, or cannot sleep because of financial problems, we can be sure our overseeing parents have not taken responsibility - or that they have not clearly expressed it to our inner child. Since the task is too big for our child to handle, he becomes overwhelmed and frightened. It is up to our inner parents to make wise decisions and solve any financial problems that may arise. This sometimes requires hard work, special study, or the help of financial professionals.

Your child self does not like to balance checkbooks, fill out tax forms, or keep records; only in rare cases is this considered fun.

My client, Mark, told me that he had not filed his income tax for several years. He said that he also had not turned in expense records to his company for reimbursement. He hated dealing with such matters, he said. Mark is an educated man who travels widely as an expert and consultant in his field. But, he had been leaving his inner child in charge of adult financial matters. Not surprisingly, his inner child avoided obvious adult responsibilities - then lived in constant fear of the results.

Sam, another client, is the head of a major department at one of the large universities in Dallas. He refuses to take charge of his financial matters and, therefore, stays very stressed. For our inner parents to take charge of financial matters, a concrete decision, culminating in ongoing action, is absolutely necessary.

Several years ago, I got involved in some rather large real estate transactions. However, before I signed any contracts, I had a talk with "little Larry". I told him that no matter what happened he would always have food, clothing, a house, transportation, and his medical needs would be met. I told him that if bankruptcy became necessary as a last resort to alleviate a lifetime of financial stress, I would be willing to file. During the next six years, I went through some financial transactions I never dreamed this Arkansas boy would do. There were times when I had enormous indebtedness with no way to pay, but I never missed a night's sleep and never had to file bankruptcy. However, during that period I made certain to talk to "little Larry", regularly restating my parental commitment to him.

Ashley owned his own business but could not keep a positive cash flow. Unable to pay his bills, he finally had to close his store. Ashley grieved and felt guilty, helpless and depressed. He felt that he was a "bankrupt human being". I worked with him on not making the bankruptcy into a personal failure. Although his business had failed, he was none the less valuable as a human being. He must not reject his little boy, when "little Ashley needed his loving inner parent the most. By reclaiming his own worth as a person, Ashley was able to regain his self-esteem, and is now managing a very successful retail store.

**Steps In Handling Financial Matters:**

1. Financial responsibility begins and ends with our inner parent. Children like to spend money, but they do not like to tend to details.

2. Make a commitment to your inner child that you will provide for his or her basic needs, as well as needs for toys and for play.

3. The decision to be responsible never comes

from the child. Never ask the child to do what only the adult parents can do.

4. Be willing and ready to educate yourself financially by reading, attending seminars, seeking expert advice, etc., in order to carry out your commitment to your child.

5. Set specific times to work on finances and perform as scheduled.

6. Never work on finances at mealtime, bedtime, or when being emotionally or physically intimate.

7. Keep your priorities in order. Money is never more important than the love and happiness of your inner child.

**4. Disappointments Related To Losses**

So far in this section, I have been alluding to a form of loss: loss of health or loss of money. Now I wish to deal more directly with the feelings of grief that go along with any loss.

No look of sadness exceeds the look on the

face of a child who cannot find his favorite toy or stuffed animal. The feeling of disappointment can range from mild to extreme. The screaming, crying child's loss may seem minor to his parents, but the child is experiencing heavy trauma. So the unsympathetic parent, who responds casually or even angrily, "Don't worry about it. It will show up sooner or later " is adding to the painful feelings of loss.

Two years ago I walked out of my office to go home. I went to where I had parked my van, and not finding it there, I thought someone was playing a trick on me. No trick; it was stolen! I just stood there in shocked disbelief, my little boy becoming first frightened, then angry. I wanted to catch the person who took it, and make him pay. The emotional cost to me was very heavy, although the van was eventually found and restored, and the missing personal items were covered by insurance. A year later I left my office for the day, and saw a strange man start up my van and drive off. I was furious, but once again, helpless. Once more the van was recovered and restored. Early one morning, six months later, I walked out of my house to discover a window in the van had been broken, and some personal items had been taken from inside. A few months later, someone stole the rims off my van's wheels, and even more recently the license plates were stolen. I don't know who was now more upset me or my insurance company! Loss is never an easy thing to deal with, but one thing is sure - a sympathetic, caring, loving attitude toward our inner feeling child is always necessary when we, or our property, have been violated.

Several years ago my office was burglarized, and I grieved the loss of many important items. A client of mine recently had his office burglarized, and the loss was so great that his business almost went under. For awhile, he did not have the equipment necessary to keep it operating. We spent many hours processing through his fear and anger, concentrating as well on his need to remain powerful in order to be assertive enough to deal effectively with his insurance company.

One of my clients felt so violated when her house was burglarized, she sold it and purchased another home. She was left with the feeling that her house had been contaminated.

Whether it is loss by theft, loss of money in a bad business deal, or loss by misplacing an item, we grieve. Whether it is thousands of dollars worth of jewelry stolen, or a favorite ballpoint pen misplaced, we grieve. The tear in the corner of a child's eye says, "Pay attention to your feelings!" The harsh reality of loss cannot be stopped, but the warm comfort of attention, care, compassion, and wise decision-making can provide soothing help.

## Grieving Losses

1. Shock is generally the first feeling in loss and needs immediate attention.

2. Don't make fun of yourself or anyone else who is having a hard time with a loss. Children don't handle being made fun of very well, particularly when they are experiencing the occurrence of a loss.

3. Anger is a part of grieving and needs to be processed but don't do something stupid-- like seeking revenge or kicking a tree. That is likely to add new problems along with the loss.

4. Discuss efforts to recover or compensate for losses with your inner child. (Remember that information is not automatically transferred from our rational mind to our feelings.) Repeat your efforts until you are sure that your inner child has heard you.

5. Parenting your child calls for taking steps to minimize future losses, e.g., I now chain the steering wheel of my van to the seat.

## III - Problems Related to Self

### Self-esteem

Self-esteem cannot be earned, nor does it have to be! A child, who keeps trying to be "better", so that his parents will love him, is doomed to fail. The child's good behavior may have a favorable effect on his parents but never total enough, or permanent enough, to cause the child to feel loved. Moving from an unloved feeling to a loved feeling can only occur when we learn to love ourselves. Often it is not until we have long been residing in adult-looking bodies that this growth happens for us.

Diane, fourteen years old, was a straight "A" student, cheerleader, president of her class as well as of several clubs, and in the youth choir at church. She was a model Christian, with loving parents, but Diane was anorexic. She weighed 69 pounds when she first came to see me. She liked me and was willing to cooperate, although with some reluctance, to a gradual increase of calories. Slowly, she gained weight, into the 70s, 80s, 90s and finally passed 100 pounds. In fact, eventually she got up to 113 pounds.

Several months passed and all was well. She was proud of her weight and shape, but something happened. She started to lose weight again. It was not until recently that I discovered she had a significant problem with self-esteem. She was not perfect and although she was "almost" so, she was unable to feel complete acceptance of herself. She had been re-baptized the summer before, to assure herself that she was a Christian. She had made cheerleader again. Her grades were all "A's". But, Diane still did not feel right. The message she gave herself said:

"Your stomach is too big. You eat too much." She started eating 1,000 calories or less each day, and dropped down below 100 pounds, again. Since Diane did not feel fully accepted in spite of her excellent performance the only reason she could think of to account for her feelings was her weight. She did not feel better if she lost weight but she felt guilty if she gained. Diane can never arrive at a satisfactory weight because weight is not her problem. Her problem is her lack of good self-esteem- - which she thinks it is only possible to correct if she loses weight.

I told a physical trainer recently, that if people were hoping to gain self-love by making their bodies look a certain way, they were doomed to fail. There is nothing we can do to our looks, personality, or position that will make us have a high self-esteem. We cannot earn self-esteem because self-esteem is based on belief not on behavior. We live saturated by a culture that makes looks, performance and position the basis of human worth. No wonder we are so confused. We are human beings, not human doings! Being born gives us full membership into the human race. We are never more than, or less than, other human beings.

As children, we become confused. We think restraints and put-downs mean that we are "bad". Unable to make a distinction between who we are and what we do, we become convinced that criticisms are aimed at us personally, rather than at our actions.

Some parents also get confused. They say, "What's wrong with you? Rather than, "What you're doing is wrong." They assume that a child's "bad" behavior comes from a "bad" child.

Unconditional love means we may place conditions on the child's behavior, but not on the child's being. We love him in spite of his unacceptable behavior. No parent has ever perfected unconditional love, although some come closer than others.

Perfectionist parents demand behavior beyond a child's capabilities which guarantees failure. Consequently, the child will have a low self-esteem. On the other hand, parents who verbally exaggerate the status of their children, create an identity impossible to live up to. This, also, guarantees failure and therefore creates a low self-esteem.

Reclaiming parental acceptance will not heighten our self-esteem. That happens only by changing our beliefs about ourselves. A list of requirements can never achieve what only faith can do. Believing in ourselves calls for a faith that leaps over every feeling of shame, guilt, and self-rejection - and permission for that faith has to originate in ourselves.

Once we agree to love ourselves, then our behavior will reflect that love. Instead of good behavior producing love, love produces good behavior. Just as putting the cart in front of the horse will not work, neither will reversing the position of "love" and "behavior". Love is the motivating power that produces good actions, not the other way around. Good self-esteem precedes achievement. With a high self-esteem, enjoying and celebrating achievements naturally follows.

The day I received my doctorate, I remember I felt depressed. The reason I felt depressed was that after all my work and achievement, I did not feel any increase in my self-worth. If I had already had a high self-esteem, I could have celebrated my accomplishment. But most often, achievement for any person with low self-esteem will only increase the depression because in spite of all expectations, we still feel no better about ourselves.

We may find encouragement, but not conversion, in outside acceptance. We cannot go from low self-esteem to high self esteem because we have "achieved". We do so because of our belief. No child should ever have to perform in order to draw the love of his parents. Parental love must be as close to unconditional as is humanly possible.

## Essential Steps In Gaining Self-Esteem

1. As with most solutions, the first step is recognizing and identifying the problem.

2. It's near impossible to pull yourself up by your own bootstraps. You have to get a clear picture of yourself as a small child.

   a. Study photographs of yourself as a child.
   b. Try to visualize remembered scenes of yourself as a child.
   c. Ask your parents and others about what you were like as a child.

3. As an adult parent, you must stand between any criticism you ever heard from your parents and the image you have created for yourself of your small child.

4. You now commit to loving your child unconditionally, without any Ok from your parents. Visualize your inner child and tell him of your unconditional love.

5. Your inner child faces a decision between

continuing to seek his childhood parents' blessings, or turning to you for inner parenting.

6. Your unconditional love and your child's willing response, complete the beginning of a healthy self-esteem.

**Note:** You may require the help of a psychotherapist in order to do this, particularly if you have made a habit of "shutting yourself off' from feelings that were common to your childhood.

## Self-Discipline

Left alone, the child does not make the decision to clean his room, brush his teeth, take a bath, etc. Those decisions are made by the parents and passed on to the child. When the inner mother and father decide to take responsible action, independent of the child's wishes, that is self-discipline.

Only recently did I acknowledge that even today the "little Larry" within me no more liked to do dishes, clean house, or mow the yard than he did when he was 10 years old. I do those things not because I want to, but because my inner parents make me. Even now as I sit here writing, my little boy wants to watch a football game, or ride horses, or work on the stereo in my van, or - the list goes on. "Little Larry" feels almost mistreated that he has to write.

John, a 20-year-old man who lived with his father, could not seem to get himself up in the morning. When he finally did make it out of bed, he would watch TV most of the day. Finally, his father said, "Either get a job or move out."

Even then John did not take action. John's father came to me. "I don't know what to do about John's lack of motivation," he said. Even though John wanted to change, and in spite of his father's threats, he still lacked the motivation.

I explained to John and his father that John's inner little boy was running his life. "Just as when you were a little boy," I told John, "and your mother had to get you up, there is now a mother inside you that will have to get you up, today. Your little boy will never change. He won't ever want to get up! There is another part of you that needs to move into action - to take charge." John looked at me with a puzzled look, and then he said, "What do I do?" "You make a decision that at a certain time you will get up even at the protest of your little boy." I suggested. "You hear a voice saying, Son, you will get up regardless of how you feel.' But then be kind to your little boy. Tell him you love him and promise to take good care of him all day long. It's almost as if his inner daddy tells him to get up and his mother rubs his back as he sits on the side of the bed, helping him to get awake. TV is never an option. He does not think, 'Well, do I want to watch TV or listen to my stereo?' A decision has already been made. The inner parents both make and enforce a decision. Once the decision is made, carrying it out is not up for a vote.

"I go to the spa to exercise five times a week. The mornings when I go, I never think, 'Well, am I going to work out this morning or not?' because that decision has already been made by my parent-self. I simply carry out a pre-planned course of action."

Well, John not only got the point, he got up and got a job and is continuing to maintain a high level of discipline because he no longer leaves the running of his schedule to his little boy. Before I sound too unsympathetic with the child who desires to play, I must acknowledge that surely a balance between work and play is necessary. I told my little boy that after I write for two hours, we will go play golf. The promise lessened his resistance. I recommend that you work on tradeoffs between your inner parents and your inner child. But if you let your inner child plan for all of your time, someone else will have to feed and clothe you.

**Steps To Achieve Self - Discipline**

1. Look at the way you spend your time and see if your inner parent or your inner child determines your schedule.

2. Assess your priority list to see if you are giving proper time to the things at the top.

3. Be sympathetic and loving to your child as you plan to do necessary things that may not

be fun for him. Explain that properly taking care of those "unfun" things creates more freedom to thoroughly enjoy the fun things when it's their time.

4. Trade-off work and playtime with your child. Relieve lengthy work periods with playful intermissions.

5. Action is the test of a genuine decision. Wanting to get something done is different from getting it done.

**Self-Abuse**

For various reasons and in various ways, people are often self-destructive. Let me tell you about three different people.

Ann was obese. Her husband had left her with three children and no child support. She was hurting from rejection and from the struggle of supporting and caring for her three small children. In her pain and hassle with the situation, Ann put on extra pounds.

I asked her to bring a picture of herself

when she was younger and weighed less. She was beautiful in the picture. Ann had given up the hope that life could ever be any better for her than it was now. Without any future relief in sight, she fed herself as if she were feeding a child who cried all the time, hoping something would work to stop the crying. Every week she unsuccessfully promised to eat less.

Ann had grown up with a father who was a minister and who was very strict with her. She never could please him. Then, predictably, she married a man she could not please. Now she had made transference to me.

She worked hard in therapy and made some nice gains but resisted the idea of being a loving daddy to herself. Finally, one day I told her I could not make her change. She would have to take the responsibility herself. She started crying, said I didn't believe in her anymore, and left very upset. Ann never came back, but her daughter and one of her friends told me that she had gone on a program of weight loss and lost so much weight that she was looking and doing great.

Mike was on drugs and alcohol. When his wife learned that he had been molesting their daughter, she made him leave the house and subsequently filed for divorce. Mike was miserable. He came to me on two occasions feeling hurt, anger and extreme guilt. Mike took his own life. During one of his sessions with me, Mike had confided that he was not wanted by his mother, and she had even told him so. In fact, when he was eleven years old attending his father's funeral she riled, "If you had never been born, I would have had more time with your father." Mike was angry at being alive. In a final attempt to please his mother, Mike ended his life on his birthday. But for Mike, suicide was only the last in a series of self-abusive acts throughout his life.

Charles had a problem with sexual addiction. Every weekend he cruised the clubs looking for a new woman with whom to have sex. Not only was he unable to establish a meaningful relationship, he was running the risk of catching a deadly disease. But for Charles, filling the void in his life was worth the risk. With little regard for his emotional or physical health, Charles had various sexual encounters with women friends, went to X-rated movies, and read porn magazines routinely each week. During one therapy session I said, "Charles, the woman you are looking for is the woman inside of you." Big tears started streaming down his cheeks.

The thing that Ann, Mike, and Charles had in common was the need to harm themselves. More than just hurt by a low self esteem, they were angry at themselves and cared not at all about the abuse they were experiencing. A vicious cycle was created: Wanting to be free of pain, they sought relief in food, drugs and sex. But, instead of experiencing relief their pain was increased. The only solution they imagined would release them from their pain, was to convert their parents into loving caring people, and this they felt would never happen.

I have observed, in working with addictions and sex abuse in any form, that these individuals have inside them a child who never felt loved by his parents. Even if their parents did in fact love them, they were unable to receive the love and the results are still the same. The real hope for the addicted individual is to discover his own inner parents, who can then become the loving parents he always wanted.

## Steps To Deal With Self-Abuse

**Note**: For a very serious condition, these steps are over simplified. In most cases, a therapist is necessary as well as support groups.

1. Accept that problems exist "The fact is, I am addicted to ________."

2. Become aware that there is a child inside you that is hurting. That hurting child within will need to express and release the pain. Regression therapy or primal therapy can have very positive healing value.

3. Ask yourself if you were a parent to a small hurting child, would you offer him alcohol, drugs, sex or cram food into him for his pain or bring any other harm to him?

4. Do what any good parent would do for his

hurting child, love him to learn the cause of h

5. The beginning of pain is abanc parents but the ultimate pain is self-abandonment. Therefore, reclaiming the chi relieves the pain.

6. Dedicate yourself to being good parents to your child, then convince him that you will be the parents he always wanted.

7. Healthy love prevents letting harm come to your child. (Remember that in self-anger, Sally threw her doll down and tried to tear the doll apart but after she made the decision to love herself she clothed her doll and wrapped her up warmly on a cold night.)

**Self-Forgiveness**

The ultimate relief is self-forgiveness. Forgiveness is another word for renewal or a new beginning. Forgiveness honors the old expression, "Today is the first day of the rest of your life."

The reason I am including self-forgiveness

here is because it has everything to do with self-esteem, self-discipline, and self-abuse. The criticism and rejection we feel as a child sets up the conditions for low self-esteem, self-abuse, and lack of discipline. Criticism and rejection form something like a cancer between the developing inner parents and the inner child. The inner parents fail to properly develop and therefore the child is left without protection to defend against an overbearing conscience.

Here forgiveness does not imply guilt. Forgiveness is permission to clean the slate of condemnation and do away with guilt. When the inner parents are mature enough to stand between the consciences and the child, and say to the child, "I love you just as you are and I will not allow your conscience to drag up anything from your past," then forgiveness has taken place.

Very often the inner child has anger toward the Inner parents for not taking better care of him. Even if inner mom and dad were incapable of taking care of the child, nevertheless, the child may have resentment. Asking the child's forgiveness for not taking better care of him is in order.

As the child forgives the parents and the parents forgive the child, a bonding occurs between them. The resulting level of intimacy provides momentum and energy to face almost anything. Just as in the biblical parable of the prodigal son's return, a celebration is in order.

## Steps Toward Self-Forgiveness

1. The inner mom and dad challenge the unreal condemnation and rejection, from the conscience toward the child.

2. Mom and dad embrace the child with unconditional love and inform the child that his past is all forgiven.

3. The child forgives his parents for not taking better care of him.

4. In order to maintain bonding, forgiving and "making- up" between your parents and your child, the process will need to be periodically repeated throughout the rest of your life.

## IV -- Problems Related To Death

### Death of a Pet

I once heard Dr. Carl Whitaker, a renowned family therapist, say that when he was eleven years old his father had killed his dog. This dog had been his companion since Dr. Whitaker was age three, and now the dog was old and very ill and the killing was necessary. However, Dr. Whitaker remarked that only recently did he realize he had not felt affectionately close to a dog since that time, when he was eleven. His story recalled to me how, similarly, when I was twelve years old my father had shot my dog, Trixie, because Dad was afraid that Trixie might have gotten rabies from some stray dogs. I remember thinking how unfortunate it was that Dr. Whitaker had not been able to again feel close to a dog, but I failed to realize until several hours later that I too have not felt close to a dog since that incident when I was twelve years old.

The death of a pet can have a profound

effect on a child or on an adult. As a child, I grieved the loss of many pets, which forced me, very early in life, to face the issue of death itself. The questions of "Why do things die?" and "Then will I die?" would repeatedly surface.

Our attachment to animals is easily understandable. Pets often express gratitude for any attention we give them. Our family now has a dog that would rather be stroked than eat. Also, pets are almost unconditionally loyal; they just keep coming to us with a friendly, loving and accepting disposition.

Joy had a little Schnauzer that was with her for fifteen years. She took great care of that dog treating it like it were her child. Joy lived alone with her dog as her companion and dreaded the day he would die. Finally, he became so ill she had to put him put to sleep. Joy had a casket made and arranged for a burial place where she could plant flowers over his grave. Recently, when she was jilted by a boyfriend, she said in anger, during a session, "Joe should have died instead of my little dog." Well, neither Joy nor I believe that animals are more important than people, but you can understand the spirit of her feelings.

The grief process with pets is the same as with any loss: difficulty in accepting the reality of the death; pain, anger, guilt, etc. All these emotions Joy is now working through so that she can finally accept the loss of her pet. Throughout this process the child inside us needs the presence of mom and dad. I still vividly remember the aloneness that I felt when I walked down into the woods where my father had shot "Trixie."

When a little neighbor girl's dog was run over by a car, I suggested that we conduct a funeral service. The neighbors gathered in her back yard as we buried her dog. Everyone went by and hugged her as she stood crying.

Your inner mother and dad need to embrace you, giving you needed support, as you share your grief with others. Don't block your feelings as Dr. Whitaker and I did. Complete your grief process so you can once again love.

## Death of a Friend

Richard was terminally ill with cancer. One Sunday afternoon, I arrived at his room for a visit and found the bed freshly made. Not immediately comprehending the meaning of the scene, I was informed by the nurse that he had died. Physically I felt sick, and emotionally I broke down in tears. Only a day or so before we had laughed together and embraced. I felt more childlike than parent like, but I could feel my inner mom and dad embracing and soothing me.

I remember standing with Bob's wife beside his bed as he opened his eyes, lifted his hand in a wave, then drew his last breath. Once again, I became physically ill and emotionally overwhelmed. Once again my inner mom and dad held and soothed me.

The loss of a friend calls for heavy-duty inner support from our mom and dad-selves. As an adult, I thank God for that inner support but when I was in the fourth grade and my friend drowned, I felt very alone because my inner parents had not yet developed. I could not communicate my grief to my childhood mother and father and, as a result, I carried unprocessed feelings inside me for years. Recently, I visited my friend's grave and, in the quiet, I experienced a peace that I find difficult to describe. I realized that the visit had allowed me to complete my grieving under the loving care of my inner mother and father.

George had served in Vietnam and he related this story to me during a session. He and his best friend were standing on a platform. His friend spotted the enemy, about to fire, and he pushed George off the platform. Unfortunately, the friend was shot and killed during the process. "I have felt guilty ever since." George cried, "I feel I do not deserve to live." George might have spent his entire life beset by feelings of guilt but, through much anger and pain, he became able to express his deep gratitude to his friend and tell him goodbye. All through the process George was held in the loving embrace of his inner mom and dad.

## Death of Our Parents

Bill had been in therapy several months when he called to tell me that his mother had died. Of course he was upset, but there was a level of adult maturity in his voice. Bill had worked a great deal on distinguishing his childhood mother from his inner mother. He told me over the phone that he was upset but did not feel abandoned or alone. "The mother inside me is very much alive," Bill said. Later, during a session he talked about, and painfully grieved, his mother's death.

Sometimes our most dreaded fear of a parent's death is that we will then become orphans. For those who operate mostly from the child position, orphaned is exactly how you feel when a parent dies. Another fear is that parents will die without giving their full approval. Many people, whose parents have died, suffer deep depression because now they never can receive their parents' blessing. Now all hope of that ever happening is gone.

Ross went to his mother's grave every day, for many days after she died. He fantasized killing about himself on top of her grave. All his life Ross had believed that his mother's approval would make him happy. Now with her gone, he believed his chance of happiness was gone also. He might as well end it all. Ross still could not connect with the comfort and blessing of his inner mother; that inner mother whose love and approval could release him to happiness if only he would receive it.

A friend of mine was in his sixties when his ninety-seven year old father died. He said that when he walked into the room and saw his Dad's still body on the bed, he said to himself, "Well, Bob, now you are going to have to grow up and learn to take care of yourself."

Losing a family member certainly does reshape something about how life feels. Even with both inner mom and dad loving and supporting us through the grief, life is made different. For some of us, the pain helps expand the dimension and quality of life, for others the pain leads us to become weaker. To all, a mystery occurs which I cannot explain.

## Death of Self

Some philosophers tell us we can't really experience life until we view life as gone. To see the end of life, then reverse our vision until it reaches the moment in which we again live, can have a profound effect.

A lawyer friend of mine says that invariably, when he is drawing up a will, the person will say, "If I die". My friend interrupts and says, "You mean when I die." The inevitability of death means that the inner mother and father cannot promise the child that they can keep the child alive. Elizabeth Kuebler Ross, who has done extensive studies on death and dying, says children handle the notion of death better than adults. The role of the inner parents is to give quality of life, not guarantee of life, to the child.

Parents used to teach children this popular prayer:

> Now I lay me down to sleep
> I pray the Lord my soul to
> keep.
> If I should die before I wake
> I pray the Lord my soul to
> take.

It is my prayer that parents will no longer teach their children to use that prayer. It is not our role to constantly frighten our children about death or the inevitability of it. The role of inner mom and dad should be to give loving support and consolation to our child's questions about death.

I felt all-alone in facing the question of death as a child. I never talked with anyone about it and no one ever talked with me. After I was 18 years old, I mentioned to my mother that I was very frightened of death. She in turn told my grandmother who got upset with me because I lacked faith in God. But, no matter how much faith I placed in God I still felt very afraid to die.

Only recently did I come to understand my fear. I knew I wanted to live to achieve success in life and enjoy having a family

> and seeing my children grow up. But, there was another issue, I was afraid of dying alone. The thought of having an accident while I was playing in the woods, and dying there all alone, was horrifying to me. Until one day, my inner mother and daddy took me in their arms and said, "Son, you will never die alone. We will be there holding you and loving you until the last moment, then we shall all go together." Since that time my anxiety about my own death has gone away.

**Conclusion**

Problems will always be a part of life. In this world there is no problem-free place to hide. Obviously, we need to have the wisdom to minimize our problems, but even the wisest person who ever lived faced some difficulties some of the time. Facing these unavoidable difficulties calls for internal unity. The individual who argues with himself when experiencing internal conflict, whose inner parents and inner child cannot get together or get along, will have a hard time coping with life's problems. But the person who is bonded in the love between his inner parents and inner child will find peace and freedom even in the presence of difficulties.

The apostle Paul, in his letter to the Romans asked, "Who can separate us from the love of God? Can trouble do it, or hardship or persecution or hunger or poverty or danger or death? No, in all these things we have complete victory through Him who loved us."

It is impossible for a person to love himself too much, for we are invited to love ourselves as God loves us. And certainly we could never love ourselves more than God loves us. So then, if we love ourselves unconditionally, neither anxiety, guilt, depression, anger nor accidents, illness, financial problems, personal struggle-not even death-can separate us from ourselves. The person bonded by self love and God's love can face anything.

# CHAPTER 7: SELF-PARENTING AND RELATING TO OTHERS

Until now, I have implied that a person with loving inner parents and a happy free inner child is self-sufficient. It may sound as if this autonomous person would need no one. Wrong. The paradox of living is that we can take care of ourselves—NO— we need others. This chapter is about needing and relating to others in a rewarding way.

A woman, who generally brought her pre-school daughter with her to the health spa, stepped on the elevator alone. When I inquired about her daughter, she said, "She's in pre-school. I take her there because that's her only chance to be with other children. She needs to play and to be with other kids." Parental love and wisdom says, "My child needs to be with others." The recluse, the loner, even the passive person is neglecting his inner child.

A person with healthy self-love will automatically love and appreciate other people. If we truly love ourselves as human beings, then we will love other human beings. No one person can be an island of love. We are unavoidably linked to others. If we attempt to avoid or hate them, then self-love deteriorates. You can't love a child and keep him away from other children. The pain that goes with self-isolation is unavoidable. A lyric from a Simon and Garfunkel song is wrong when it says, "I am a rock, I am an island, a rock feels no pain." This is simply not true, pain is inevitable, either the pain of isolation or the risk of pain when we love others.

A French philosopher, Jean Paul Sartre, said, "Hell is other people." Another French philosopher, Marcel, said, "Heaven is other people." Once again, that choice resides in whether or not our inner parents love and embrace our little child. With that as our basic commitment - i.e., that we will never betray ourselves no matter what others do--we are free to move toward others. This means that we seek to love and be intimate with others and constantly strive to improve our ability to do that. With our inner child embraced in mom and dad's love, let us continue to move toward other people.

## I - Other People

### Regression

Most children respond to attention. People in stores and restaurants interact openly with babies; there seems to be an open invitation from baby, that is, until people repeatedly hurt baby, and baby begins to retreat. The pain-pleasure ratio determines whether baby will grow up to interact freely with others or to withdraw.

Painful regressed feelings of childhood can determine how a person presents himself to others. Therapy is often needed to relieve the pain and to open us to healthy relationships. If our childhood experiences were mostly filled with pleasure, and little pain, change is unnecessary. We can simply delight in the majority of our encounters with other people.

Generally when difficulties cause one to become a scared, regressed child in the presence of others, I do "image work" therapy with him/her.

Eloise was afraid to go into malls and

supermarkets. During several sessions she projected images of her inner child, with her inner mom holding one hand and dad holding the other. I mentally walked her around in the supermarket then asked her how she felt once she captured the real presence of her inner parents, her fear disappeared. Eloise had been greatly frightened when she spent time in an orphanage as a child. With a sense of parental presence, Eloise got over her fear of being orphaned and people ceased to be a threat to her.

On the other hand, I have a friend who never meets a stranger. He converses with people in elevators and restaurants and talks with clerks in stores as if he has known them for years. As far as I know, no one has ever harmed him or been mean to him. His trust in people seems to win them over. They simply enjoy him. My friend is often regressed into his happy free child.

## Dependency

People who present themselves to others

wearing a T-shirt that reads, "Take Care of Me!" generally have a hard time in relationships. When a child walks into a crowd, we expect the crowd to watch out for the child. But when an adult acts like a child, instead of the crowd taking care of him, they generally turn away - either embarrassed or angry. People do not want to feel responsible for "adult" children. Anyway, we each have our own inner child for whom we need to care.

I have timberland in Oklahoma. A few years ago a man called to purchase my timber. I did not bother to educate myself about logging or the cost of timber. He made me an offer to which I replied, "I am not informed on such matters but I trust you to pay me a fair price." About a month later I received a call from another man who offered me twice that amount. I was furious. I called the first man, who had already started cutting the timber, and said, "You did not offer me fair market value, as I believed you would "to which he replied, " It's not my job to inform you about such matters. I'm a businessman trying to get the best deal I can." I realized then, I had presented myself to him as a child and expected him to take care of me in the business world. I had not been willing to do adult research and, thereby, properly parent my own inner child.

The world is not set up to take care of adult-age children. Much individual and group suffering is due to lack of self-parenting. People who were not properly parented as children, or who have not developed due to physical problems, are at the mercy of society. Some of these people must be parented by society through government programs, churches and various benefit organizations. But for those individuals who learn self-parenting and become self-responsible, the freedom from being dependent can be a real relief.

Barbara Streisand sang, "People who need people are the luckiest people in the world." From all I've been saying, that seems untrue; but the other side of the paradox says people who enjoy people, people who love people and let people love them, people who interact with people, have a positive, not a dependent, need for people.

## Criticism and rejection

It is impossible to live among others without rejection and criticism. People will honk at you on the road and even throw you obscene gestures no matter how carefully you drive. If you are not in charge of driving then you don't feel the abuse. That's why your inner mom and dad need to do the driving and let your feeling child ride in the back seat.

A serious problem results from criticism if it is taken as a real statement about who you are. When you alter your self-identity because of other people's opinions, you are in a scary, vulnerable position. Criticism may be their statement about your behavior but it is not a judgment of your personal value and identity.

Once you accept yourself as valuable and become clear and firm about your identity, you are ready to hear constructive criticism - which can be a learning experience if your adult parents have the wisdom to accept and process it.

A few years ago I had a house built. The bricklayer had grown up in Germany and moved to the United States as a young man. He said he struggled with the English language and would ask people to criticize his speech. But, for fear of offending him they would say, "Oh, your English is good." His reaction was, "They didn't understand how desperate I was for help." So he learned by watching a lot of television and reading the paper, but he got no help from others.

When you are secure with the care and protection of your inner parents, criticism need not harm you. It could even help.

## Communication

When my niece was a baby, she would cry out and my sister would run to her. My sister would check her out but couldn't find anything wrong; she had no open pin sticking her, she did not need a diaper change, she was not hungry. My sister wondered what in the world could be the matter, until one day she caught a glimpse of her two year old son sneaking up to the baby bed, pinching his sister and then running to hide. He was not old enough or understanding enough to express, "I really feel hurt that I have been replaced, that I don't get all the attention. I don't like sharing."

This behavior is understandable for a child, but when adults don't go direct with their feelings, relationships break down. Honesty and reality are synonymous. Acknowledging our inner child's hurt and acting on it is essential to successful relationships. Wisdom and discretion are necessary in communicating our inner feelings, but to deny those feelings will distort the meaning of a relationship. If we do not deal directly with feelings, our inner child will find ways to communicate anger in areas unrelated to the real issue.

A client called me crying and screaming into the phone. Finally, I understood that her boyfriend had been shot to death. He had been depressed and angry at the world. He traveled with a pistol in his car. Somehow, another driver had done something to draw his anger and he shot at the other man. It happened that the other man also had a pistol and fired back. Both men were killed in the shootout. What started as unidentified and unprocessed feelings of anger became misdirected action, and tragedy resulted.

On the other hand, there are positive emotions, which may not easily be communicated. Gifts, flowers and cards can be the very beautiful means for communicating appreciation. But, one may not choose to tell a group, or an individual, how very much he loves them for fear of deep emotions welling up and creating overwhelming intimacy. He may be embarrassed to allow his inner child the freedom to show his true feelings. However, those people who allow themselves the freedom to risk expressing their deep love, generally stir that same deep emotion in very appreciative recipients.

To give an honest report of what we are feeling, we must be well acquainted with our inner child. Our inner parents need to listen to what the child is feeling, and take the responsibility to put it into words. Telling someone our true feelings makes us feel real, connected, and together. Conversely, saying that we feel happy when in fact we feel sad is being unreal. That unreality causes neurosis, anxiety, depression and broken relationships. We can enjoy life and be successful only in the realm of reality. The honest acknowledgment and reporting of our feelings is our reality.

## Receiving Love

Letting others love us is essential to happiness,-our's and their's. Earlier I made many appeals for you to love yourself, i.e., your inner child. If you do not love your inner child, you will not let others love him either. The child who does not feel love is the saddest child in the world.

Loving others is a beautiful and wonderful expression of life. However, if there were no people willing to receive love, this world would be a terrible place. People become very frustrated trying to love people who do not love themselves. Feeling rejection is difficult and so is feeling that our love is rejected.

It has been a long time since I've seen Beth, but I will never forget the first night she came to group therapy. She instantly went to the corner of the room and pulled the drape over her. Beth had been molested by three different stepfathers. While working as a motorcycle police person she had been hit by a car and seriously injured. As a teenager she had a child, which she gave up for adoption. At that time, she preferred the lesbian lifestyle. During the session, she ran out of my office, but I caught her in the waiting room. I said, "I don't want you to go." She said, "Why?" I said, "Because I love you." Her rigid body relaxed as she slowly sat down.

She stayed in the group for several months screaming out the remembered pain of her childhood and learning to love her inner child. Shortly after therapy, she married and had a little girl. The primary value of therapy is for people to experience the joy of self-love and the meaning and fulfillment of letting others love them.

## Giving Love

Small children may be self-centered but they can also be very giving. At a family reunion, I marveled at my four year old niece as she responded to my two year old nephew, who was crying, by putting her arms around him, patting him on the back and asking, "Are you alright?"

A client told me that her four year old daughter said, "Mother I will quit sucking my thumb if you will quit smoking cigarettes" because she was concerned about her mother health.

Doing for others is not just a sacrificial commitment. It is a natural outgrowth of healthy self-love. To truly love ourselves means we love everything that being a human means, which includes loving other human beings. The love of others must include self and the love of self must include others. To put self above others is narcissistic and to put others above self is masochistic.

A truly loving mother will not give her little child the last piece of apple pie. Rather she will halve it, giving half to herself (her inner child) and half to her little son or daughter. And, she will enjoy the intimacy of loving both children as they sit and enjoy eating apple pie together.

By taking care of our inner child, we are ready to love, and to consider the needs of others. Failure to do so neither takes care of our inner child, or others. Helping others fulfills love at its deepest level, because it completes the cycle of love: self and others, others and self. Despite all the news about crime, I am still most deeply moved by the acts of love, kindness and help, which occur everyday. Little Jessica's rescue from the well, in Midland, Texas, several years ago was not merely a rescue but a metaphor of human love.

## II -- Relating to people at work

### Regression

We generally relate to each other at work in the same manner we related to the family members we grew up with. That is because regression means operating out of our child a great deal of the time. Bosses usually function according to the kind of authority their parents displayed, so companies become like big families. If we operate out of our child with little inner parental supervision, we will likely have a hard time in the work world.

Sometimes the authority displayed in the company will cause us to adapt and obey and become a good worker but we may not enjoy what we are doing.

"Free child" regression is welcomed in some types of work. A local radio station has what they call their "fun and games" department. Most recreational parks and sports-related work calls for "free child" participation.

**Dependence**

When we enter the work world with a high level of dependency needs we present ourselves to employers, clients and co-workers, as small children to be cared for. Few companies want to take us on to raise. Confidence comes from taking responsibility for our inner child. And, it is confidence that generally gets people hired and keeps them working.

We typically grow up with a need for family approval. Seeking approval from our fellow workers is frequently a frustrating situation, often causing us problems on the job. Ron was so nervous that it was difficult for him to work. His high intelligence and dedication to work did not help him overcome his weariness at being judged by his fellow workers. After helping him visualize the image of his loving parents holding each hand as he moved through his work as a computer programmer, he was able to overcome his fear and enjoy being around the people at work.

## Rejection and Criticism

Connie got a terrible review from her boss. She made an effort to challenge the criticism in front of the personnel director, but the director sided with her boss. This experience frightened her so much she became paranoid. When Connie came to me her speech was so rapid I could hardly understand her. Not only did she talk constantly, she wrote page after page and brought this all to me in hope that I would find a clue to her problem. I made an effort to learn all I could about her. We went over Connie's family pictures, one by one, as she told me about her life at various ages. I talked with her children and her siblings. Connie was in her early 60's, divorced, and had been hospitalized twice for a nervous disorder. She believed that her parents had loved her as their child, but that people generally had not received her well. I asked her to adopt her inner little girl and she agreed. Connie learned to nurture and protect her child self and within months she was able to return to work. The personnel director was wise enough to place her in another department where she thrived. That was years ago and recently we visited and talked, even laughed, about her condition back then.

Job trauma can be wide ranging in degree of debilitation. Thinking that the company has control of our very being, our very soul, can pose a great threat to our inner child. No one can own us. No one can take our child self away from us. Once we feel confident that our future ultimately rests only in our own hands, we can relax. In fact we can hear criticism, even experience being fired, and not get blown away emotionally.

## Communication

Indirect acting-out, occurs a lot at work. We may get mad at the boss or the company and intentionally do something that results in harm. We may be unable to verbalize anger directly because the boss may not wish to hear anger. However, if we do not deal with our anger by releasing it in a safe fashion, we can build up a tank full and explode inappropriately.

David is a quiet, rather shy man who works as an engineer for a large electronics firm in Dallas. Throughout his lengthy stay with the company, he received good reviews and enjoyed his work. That is, until a certain supervisor was placed over him.

The supervisor was a loud, overbearing, critical person who "whomped" on David for no reason. One day the supervisor walked quietly to David's cubicle and screamed, "David, what are you doing?" This shattered David's emotions so severely that he went straight to the man above his supervisor, threw his badge on the desk and quit. David went home so shaken that his wife called to ask me to see him immediately.

I was able to help David calm down and return to work, but we spent the next several sessions teaching David's inner parents to be assertive on behalf of his little boy. Finally, one day David said, "I'm not afraid of him any more." He had made a commitment never to allow that man to intimidate him again. He accepted the responsibility for speaking his feelings.

When the child does not get what feels like fair treatment, he blames others and may seek revenge, or may withdraw and blame himself. Transactional Analysis expressed it "I'm OK, you're not OK" or "I'm not OK, you're OK." Either position represents a painful life. Being able to talk with our spouse or with a friend can help. Some companies provide psychotherapists or we may need to seek help from a psychotherapist in private practice.

**The Feel of Love**

Some work situations allow for a great deal of closeness. If you happen to work in that kind of situation, you are indeed fortunate.

I observed a company that went through a transition very much like a family sometimes does. The owner was a man and the personnel director was a woman, "Dad and Mom". There were employees who acted as older brothers and sisters and who helped to oversee things. They were a close family. But when business turned bad and the company faced a financial crisis, instead of showing love for each other, they began to fight over various issues. People started quitting and instead of farewell parties as before, there were hard feelings. The original family disintegrated. I still see people who once worked for the company, as well as people who still work for the company and both have grieved the loss of the old loving family-like atmosphere.

Hopefully we will be open to enjoy love wherever people love, but we can't always count on our work place to provide it. However, we may be determined to find such a place for our inner child. Certainly it is a worthy pursuit.

### The gift of loving

People often find it difficult to love or get

involved with fellow workers. They choose to simply go to work, do their job and go home. Such makes for a lonely day but keeps down any entanglement in other people's lives. With healthy self-parenting, however, loving our fellow workers is possible. The risk of involvement with others is that we may get hurt. But when we are committed to take care of our inner child by consistently loving him, protecting him from rejection and criticism, and nurturing him through hurt, then any risk of love becomes possible. It is also in the wisdom of our inner parents that boundaries are established. How much time can we reasonably give to hearing someone tell his problems? How much emotion can we reasonably invest in another? Our wise inner parents should monitor these choices.

With parental care in place we can go forth to love and help others, adding depth and meaning to our lives. Encouraging words in passing, a note of sympathy or a pat on the back, take very little time. Your inner child will love it!

## III - Friends

## Regression (the beginning and sometimes end of friendship)

Friendships most often begin with the meeting of our inner children. A certain playfulness in someone else matches the playfulness in us. Children are naturally attracted to each other and that same natural attraction resides in adults who are attuned to their inner child.

A beautiful friendship is sustained by mature inner parents who watch over and direct the activities of the child. As two children play, both sets of parents see that they play fairly and don't hurt each other. The parents are sometimes entertained by the freedom with which the children play. Often two children do hurt each other and their parents are needed to stop them Wise parents help them to resolve their conflict and resume their play. Many friendships are broken because the inner parents are passive, therefore neglecting any attempt to solve the problem. In some cases they simply do not have the necessary skill. Friendship begins with the child inside, and will end with the child inside if not properly supervised.

## Dependency

The beauty of self-parenting is the freedom it allows us to enjoy our friends without a desperate need for them.

When my daughter was in high school, she had a friend with whom she was mutually dependent. They spent hours talking on the phone and staying at each other's homes. I remember Lisa trying to tell me just how awful life would be without her friend. Obviously that concerned me, but adolescents often develop heavy dependencies. Finally, they had a major conflict they could not resolve. They could not sustain their friendship because neither of them had enough inner parental responsibility for her own inner child - too much dependency had developed in the relationship. When the "other" failed to take care of them, each one became very angry.

Knowing how to receive someone's friendship means that we bring enough self-support so that our expectations are reasonable. Sure, that's easy to say. What's reasonable? The tension of establishing what is reasonable calls for a willingness on the part of the inner parents to oversee the friendship; for the child to listen to the inner parent's guidance, and for some trial and error experiences while seeking a healthy balance.

## Rejection and Criticism

When rejection and criticism are healthfully supervised by the inner parents, the friendship is strengthened. When my children reported feeling rejection by their friends, I appealed to them to talk about it with them. At least, seek to understand what is happening and offer a chance for reconciliation.

Criticism as I mentioned earlier can be a statement of love; a sincere desire to help. But if it is heard as rejection, then the consequence can be too great. If criticism comes our way, we need to go toward it, pursue it, seek to understand it; call for clarification. If it was intended as "help" we will know. If it was an effort to cause hurt because of issues that are unresolved, you deserve to know. If we are unable to do this, our inner parents are not taking care of us. If we have difficulty strengthening the inner parents on our own, it may be desirable to see a psychotherapist.

**Communication - Telling the truth**

One of the most exciting things about a close friendship is the freedom to tell all. Sharing very private things in the company of someone who accepts us, no matter what we say, can be a very warm and rewarding experience. It would be a rare friendship, however, that could handle a total revelation of one's most secret thoughts and feelings. That ideal generally ends in disappointment; the overseeing wise parents are seldom wise enough for all occasions.

Very often friends will communicate an expression that smacks of rejection. If the parents are not there to intervene then the friendship can be lost. The wise overseeing parent allows for looks of disapproval as due to indigestion, hemorrhoids, headaches, PMS, or any number of problems which create expressions that only look like rejection. Our inner parents will keep our child from overreacting by explaining what may be happening and by seeking verification. For example: One might say, "Your look shows disapproval. Is that how you are feeling?" If our friend responds, "I do indeed disapprove!" then we can deal directly with that position. If our friend assures you no problem exists, then the issue is over.

Telling the truth invites a reaction. But the truth can be spoken in love without sarcasm. Harsh criticism can sometimes invade the child's world before the inner parents can intervene. If that happens, rebellion is likely to occur. The response may be very unpleasant. However, to bring up an issue in a tone of love invites a tone of love. Let it be clear, however, that trying to manipulate a friend by being nice will not necessarily guarantee a pleasant response. The best position is honesty, which gives our friend the freedom to be just as honest.

**Feeling loved**

One of the gifts we can offer our friends is

the pleasure of loving us. In order to do that we open ourselves up to graciously receive their love.

Jane, a single parent, struggles to raise her children. She has had few friends and has not dated in a long time. Recently, when she came in for her session, she announced that she had given over virtually all of the past few years of her life to taking care of her children. But, now she realized it was time to make a life of her own. She said that over the past weekend she had purchased some new clothes in preparation for meeting people and, hopefully, starting to date. She told me all of this through tears of grief over the fact that her children were growing away from her. I said I was glad that finally she was taking steps to take care of herself. Then I said something that caught her totally off guard. I said, "Besides that, you've been cheating other people too long." "What do you mean?" she asked with a puzzled look. I said, "You have not given other people the pleasure of knowing you or the joy of loving you." A pleased look came across her face as she said, "You know, I never thought about it that way."

A friend of mine, who was returning from a missionary assignment in Indonesia after four years, called me from the airport. His excitement flowed through his words. I could tell he was glad to be back and was enjoying talking to me. I was happy, too. But just before the conversation was over, he said, "I love you." I was unprepared to receive his expression of feeling. I responded, "I'm sure glad you're back." I believed in his love, and I also loved him, but I did not give him the full satisfaction of truly loving me at that moment. Nor did I fully receive his love for my own pleasure.

Making ourselves available for our friends to love, and allowing that love to permeate our very soul constitutes one of the highest joys in life. One of my favorite people, and a truly great friend, is my major professor, Dr. John Newport, who was recently being honored at his retirement. A speaker at the ceremony, a former student, concluded by looking at John and saying, "John, I dearly love you," through his tears. By the look on John's face, you knew he had received his love. As I felt tears well up in my eyes,

I turned to my wife only to see the tears flowing down her cheeks. What a moment!

## The gift of love

Very often when someone does something for a friend, and the friend is overcome with gratitude, the person will say, "Well, what are friends for?". Implying, of course, that the nature and meaning of friendship is to help each other.

When I was eleven years old, my closest friend and I got into a fistfight. We had not spoken for a couple of days when my supervisor, at the newspaper office, asked me if I knew someone who wanted a paper route. Such an opportunity did not come along very often and the first person I though of was my friend. I really struggled over what to do.

But, finally I mustered up my courage and went over to his house. When I walked in he just looked at me without a word. I said, "They need someone to carry papers, do you want a route?" He quickly responded, "Sure." I stayed and we resumed playing as usual. It was only a few years later that he helped me to get a job. What are friends for?

A gift means however that we give without expecting to be repaid, and we receive without any expectation of having to repay. The joy of giving finds its reward within itself. The child knows what I mean.

## IV - Parents

### Regression

I remember when the playwright, Tennessee Williams, was being interviewed on a talk show. He said that even after all the psychotherapy he had been through, every time he got around his mother he felt like a little boy all over again.

Parents provide the strongest stimulus for regression. The way they look, sound, smell, and touch has been familiar to us since the day we were born. This familiarity takes us back through the remembered history of our life. Visiting with our parents, or talking with them on the phone, often makes us feel like children again. This poses no serious problem unless there were serious problems when we were growing up, which we have not yet resolved. If we had a happy healthy childhood, then we welcome contact with our parents.

## Dependency

The role of parents is to raise their children so the children will grow and no longer need them. If we still need our parents after we're grown, then the parenting role is incomplete. However, efforts to relate to our parents, as a child in need will, in most cases, draw the same response we got as a child.

Lois called me crying and angry because of what had just happened with her father. She said she told him she needed him to be there for her and assure her that he loved her. His only response was, "I don't understand what you're talking about."

Once more, in her 41 years of life, she felt the same lack of love and feelings of rejection. Her efforts to lean on her father for emotional support had failed again, just as her efforts to feel loved and supported by her husband and numerous men friends had failed.

Many people still call and go visit their parents hoping to get more parenting. They may get advice and may even get nurtured, but if their own inner capacity to parent themselves has not developed there will always be a level of disappointment.

I went to my hometown in Arkansas several years ago to visit with my father who lived alone, since mother was in a nursing home and mentally unaware of most things. I spent two days video taping him as he talked about family history and shared family stories. When I started to leave we embraced, and he clung to me as if not wanting me to go. I then drove by the nursing home to tell mother good-bye.

Shortly thereafter, as I drove along, I felt a tremendous gratitude welling up inside me as my little boy-self let me know he was glad I was his daddy and mother. I also realized that I had had a wonderful visit, even though my parents were beginning to depend on me.

### Criticism and rejection

Wanting to please our parents makes it difficult to deal with their criticism and rejection. Bob, who is 52 years old, refuses to call his mother because she immediately starts to criticize him. He then feels hurt and angry and begins to yell back at her and the conversation ends in disaster. Bob wants a good relationship with his mother and his mother wants a good relationship with Bob but this does not feel possible to either one at this time.

Some parents never quit trying to correct what they were unable to change when their children were small. Others, because of various strands of neurosis, would never be satisfied no matter what their children did. If our prerequisite to having a relationship with our parents is for them to be completely satisfied with us, then we may never be able to have a relationship with them. However, if we are satisfied with ourselves, then pleasing our parents is no big deal.

Our conscience is made up primarily of taped messages of our parents' criticism, a collection of their rights and wrongs. Before we can be free of them, we must redo our tapes and erase any messages we do not wish to keep. Once this has been done, we allow our own inner parents to establish our own value system. No one is truly a free person until this occurs.

As a free person, we can choose the role we wish to have with our parents. We can choose never to see them, see them occasionally, or see them often. Their criticism or rejection should not decide the course of our life or what we attempt to do in relating to them.

## Telling the Truth - It's Worth The Honesty

A client told me that every time her mother came to see her she put her down. I said, "Why don't you tell your mother what she is doing?" Her response was, "Oh, I could never do that." But finally she did, and her mother apologized and said she never realized she was doing that.

Once when I visited my dad, I told him it bothered me when he raised his voice at me. "I never realized that I raised my voice.", he said. If we are not honest with our parents, we cannot have a really honest relationship with them. When we were children, we may not have felt free to tell our parents about the things they did that bothered us. But as adults, we have the right to relate to our parents in a straight adult fashion. In fact, if we do not, our feelings will control us, and place tremendous limitations, on our relationship.

Being straightforward in telling our parents about our feelings does not mean that what we say will be graciously received - the opposite may be true. We may face serious conflict but if we don't run some risk, the relationship is seriously limited. With the wisdom of our inner parents we protect our inner child, and we are faithful to the truth. Then we speak to our parents in a tone of love.

## Letting our parents love us

I know of a family therapist who will not see anyone unless he brings his parents to therapy. I have heard him say that of all the parents he has seen, none have done other than declare love for their children. Many admitted they didn't know how to show their love, but all said they knew it was there.

When we don't get what we want as children, or what we think we need, often our hurt feelings interfere with our letting our parents love us. If we do not allow for their limitations, then we do not get to experience our parents' love in whatever capacity they are able to love.

One of the healthiest things we can do, after we remove the myths from around our parents, is to get to know them as people. By developing objectivity, we become able to touch their real humanness. To see their peculiar needs, their childishness, their weakness; as well as their creativity, their awareness, and their desire for intimacy can help us in many ways - as well as allow us a powerful and meaningful relationship with them.

Joy's father was an alcoholic who was very abusive to the family. Because he was so hateful and so disliked a member of the family actually shot and killed him when Joy was only two years old. She went to live with her father's parents until she was nine years old. When her mother was finally able to take her, she was verbally abused by her mother. When Joy first started therapy, she had great resentment for her mother. After working through a lot of negative feelings, and making the choice to be "mother" to herself, Joy began to relate to her mother differently. She told me recently about embracing her mother as her mother told Joy that she loved her very much. Joy said now that she is free from needing her, and free from her negative feelings about her, she is free to love her mother.

Earlier in this section, I may have left the impression that if we parent ourselves we don't need anything from our outer parents. In a mysterious spiritual way our parents will always occupy a unique place in our lives; a special place that always will be there. And, as parents so will we always be special to our children. We are indeed blessed if we have had the opportunity to freely love and freely receive love.

During the first 45 years of my life, my father never told me he loved me. I believed that he did but he never put it into words. During the next five years, he haltingly choked out the words. "We love all of you children." His final words to me were, "Larry, I love you very much." That was a very special, even reverent, moment. Again the paradox of relationships says: I don't need my father - yes I do.

**The gift of love**

The feeling that we need to do "things" for our parents because of all they did for us is motivation by guilt. Parenting ought not leave the child indebted to his parents; it is a responsibility taken on without asking permission of the child. If parenting is a gift of love, then we are free to give to our parents out of love.

The beauty of self-parenting is that now we are no longer in need, or under obligation to our parents - and we have become free to truly love them. One of my delights, as a therapist, is to join in the experience of freedom from their parents, that my clients attain - only to hear them speak of a renewed relationship and their joy in buying a present or card for their parents.

The day when our parents become old and need special attention, it is wonderful when we can oversee the process from our free adult inner parent and our loving inner child. As I mentioned earlier, no matter how autonomous we become, we are mysteriously linked to our parents. That link can be a joyous or a miserable one. The care, love and attention that our wise inner parents give to our inner child make it possible to work toward a positive link. The mature love of one's children can make a dying heart glad. Maybe the finest gift we can give to our parents is to be totally responsible for our inner child's well being.

## V -- Sweethearts - Husbands and Wives

### Regression

If our parents do not provide training in parenting ourselves then we either go back to them for more parenting or we seek substitute parents. A great many courtship's and marriages involve seeking substitute parents.

It just could be that some romantic feelings come from regression. Feeling an attraction for someone generally has no understandable reason. There is a mysterious element, which cannot be fully explained as only sexual. It could be that deep down, inside the child, there is the excitement of having discovered the ultimate parent. For this reason romance must continue to mature for there to be any real depth and security in the relationship. This explanation is not an effort to relegate romance to a lesser value. I treasure the feelings within the child as being worthy of our fullest respect and attention.

It is interesting that the expressions of endearment, the holding and caressing, the physical intimacy of courtship are so similar to what a baby gets. No wonder regression occurs and many immature acts take place during courtship. But it is the wise, caring, loving, and overseeing inner parents who provide for the child's fulfillment in a relationship. Most often when a couple comes in for therapy, the thing they regret most is the loss of that warm intimate closeness. The magic is gone and their inner children are feeling neglected.

There is healthy and unhealthy regression. In the healthier regression, the inner parents are aware of what is occurring and protect the child. For example, a man who is ill may want his wife to mother him. That's quite OK. But suppose he wants the mothering when he is well and she is sick. Now they have a problem.

Regression is also great for play. A couple that can play well together will never get bored with each other. Play intimacy is one of the highest levels of intimacy. Play intimacy can also be wonderful foreplay for sexual intimacy.

Regression can enhance or destroy a marriage depending on the maturity level of the inner parents.

### Dependency

Substitute parent overseers are doomed to failure. When we do not properly parent ourselves, our expectation of others will always disappoint us. No one can be with us 24 hours a day; no one can be fully understanding of our conditions and needs. In fact, the other partner will often react with anger because we are trying to take her away from the needs of her own child in order to take care of ours. Parenting ourselves allows for some dependency but the ultimate security and care must reside within.

One of the problems caused by two adult-children marrying is that they may be misled as to the marriage contract. On a visit with my parents a few years ago, Dad was very upset because he could not take care of Mother's feelings. They had been married for nearly 60 years. When they married, Dad's obligation was to make Mother happy. And Mother's plan was that he would, in fact, make her happy.

Mother was angry at my Father because he had not given her the happiness she believed he should, and Dad was angry at Mother because she wouldn't let him make her happy in his own way. It was a system sure to fail because they entered into a contract that could never be honored. Mother was not fully developed in her ability to parent herself. She did not have a good functional inner father who would oversee her; she did not have a good functional inner mother who would nurture and reassure her. She had given a great deal to her children hoping to receive back a blessing from them, along with the assurance that she was OK. Her intentions were good.

Certainly her efforts were not something she could be blamed for. She did the best she could under the circumstances, but her parents simply did not prepare her for an adult role in life. So Dad was attempting to take a little girl and make her functional, secure, safe and happy. Now Dad's problem was that he operated as a little boy feeling he has to make Mamma happy. So this was a problem of two children - each trying to make the other one happy - each being angry at the other one for refusing to be as happy as each feels he/she deserves. Taking care of our inner child releases blame and provides security.

Mack came to see me several years ago. Recently he called me and was very distraught because his wife was ill and he was afraid she was going to die. As it turned out, she had gallstones, which were medically treated and she was fine. But Mack had connected with his extreme dependency on his wife and could not see a life for himself should something happen to her. Mack had neglected to keep his inner child informed that he would be there for him no matter what happened. When I said, "Tell your little boy you will be there for him, no matter what". He immediately said, "I already feel better."

John has acted out his anger, most of his

life, in passive ways. He had spent various times in therapy with me in the past, but just hadn't been able to have a breakthrough. I attempted to get him in touch with his little boy but he could not comprehend and experience his child. Recently he came to see me in a state of distress. He had physically abused his wife and she had him put in jail. He said he could not promise that he would not do it again. He felt out of control.

Once more, I had him imagine his little boy sitting opposite, in another chair. I asked what he thought his little boy wanted and he said, "Someone to put an arm around him and tell him that everything is going to be all right." I then moved my chair over by his, laid my arm around his shoulders, hugged him and said, "Everything is going to be all right." I asked him if he would make that statement to his little boy, and he did. He made contact for the first time. It was a good session and, as he started to leave, he turned to the empty chair, reached for his little boy's hand and said, "Come on son, let's go," and walked out of the room holding his inner child in his arms. That night he told the group he had found his little boy and was going to learn how to take care of him. He also understood that his out of control behavior must change. Self assurance never makes abusive behavior OK.

Women who have been in a bad relationship sometimes say "all men are alike" and men say the same of women. They can't be trusted, they are selfish, etc. This is the reaction of a hurt child after trying to deal with another hurt child.

A client, who had been jilted, said she had made the decision never to enter into another relationship with a man. I said, "After you deal with the pain and disappointment, and become fully in charge of your little girl, and still wish to make that decision then you will be free to do so."

Excessive need means that we are not taking the responsibility for our inner child. Logic says that if we can find someone to take care of us, we will feel gratitude for his or her care. However, invariably the dependent person gets angry at their surrogate parent. They become like the rebellious teenager who feels in bondage, but cannot totally care for himself.

It was hard for me to comprehend why Mary, who couldn't drive, didn't have a job, had few outside activities and no close friends, stayed so angry at her husband. She relied on him for nearly everything but would get furious at him for no real reason. Mary was really angry at herself and hated the bondage of her dependency on George.

Too much dependency in marriage will guarantee a high level of anger, which is a sure-fire way to kill romance. When a person feels a need that he thinks the other person should tend to, but does not, he feels rejected. Rejection hurts. Hurt converts to anger. Anger causes withdrawal or attack.

The couple whose marriage is based on too much and the wrong kind of need will feel tremendous romance during the wedding and honeymoon, but at the divorce they hate each other. The romance went "south" because the marriage was based on too much need and too little response.

Need and want are often confused in a relationship. Need implies a serious limitation on life without a significant other. Want includes need but comes from a child who is expressing some natural desires. To say, "I need a woman", sounds of bondage. To say, "I desire a woman", sounds of freedom. It is more than a matter of semantics. The desperate child seeks a rescuer. The desiring child seeks a companion.

## Criticism and rejection

Most relationships begin with little or no criticism - which makes for early bliss because the courter feels he has found unconditional love. Not so. Such an illusion will someday be crushed. No person can be true to his own feelings and totally accept someone else's behavior. Unpleasant overlapping of another's territory is certain to occur.

I have known of several couples that lived together for two or three years before they got married and then got divorced less than a month after the wedding. Often a floodgate of criticism opens after the wedding because the person feels more secure and therefore freer to unleash pent-up feelings. The unprotected child simply cannot handle it.

Criticism as an act of love is very different from criticism as rejection. Criticism given as a wise choice, from the parents' love for their child, is a revelation of the inner self to the partner, which allows for deeper intimacy.

On the other hand, rejection is also possible. When it occurs, intervention by the inner parent is necessary. This is a serious event between the child world and the adult world. When little Susie comes home crying because she likes little Joey but little Joey pays more attention to Lisa, what do you say? Do you say, "Well, I guess your life is over."? Or do you say, "It sure hurts to like someone who tells you he likes someone else."? But, after awhile you won't feel so bad. Besides, you don't need Joey to make you precious or important because you already are. I will stay very close to you until the pain goes away."

What if an adult who gets rejected could hear an inner voice telling him that eventually he'll be OK? Telling him that it's OK to hurt now because in due time it will stop? That whoever it is who's rejecting him cannot be the source of his happiness or importance? Providing that reassurance is an important job of the inner parents. If the inner child listens and trusts that voice, he or she will not get depressed or be suicidal.

Even the pain of divorce can be better handled when reassurance is given to the inner child. One of my clients wrote about her experience after her divorce.

"After Susan (my daughter) left for her prom, Brad (my son) took me out to eat for Mother's Day and gave me the gift of a necklace. I was so overcome with feelings I began to cry. I had deserted my children and left them homeless. I felt as if I didn't deserve to have a good Mother's Day because I had abandoned them through the divorce. I realized I was in my child state because the pain was so great and I couldn't stop crying. I had no home for Brad and Susan, or for myself. We (Brad, Susan, and little Melinda) were all abandoned. After crying myself to sleep, I woke up at 3:00 AM and began to cry again. I just couldn't stop I lay in bed trying mentally to put the pieces together: Why was I still so upset?"

"I walked into the living room, picked up my doll (the self doll), held her close to my heart, and cried. I told her that I knew how she felt not having a home, but that we really did have a very nice place to live. I knew it was small and there wasn't room for Brad and Susan, but she was going to need to give me a little time and trust me because I was doing the best I could do right now - and in due time we would have a home large enough for all of us. I told her again of my love for her and said I would always be there for her.

"I stopped crying and began to feel very peaceful. I went back to bed and slept and had a wonderful dream which I will never forget."

## Telling the truth

To not clearly communicate with our spouse, about how we really feel can jeopardize the relationship. Rose told me she was working in her backyard doing some landscape gardening and wanted her husband, who was in the house, to help her. So, in order to let him know she wanted help, she squirted water on the window of the room he was in. When he would not come out to help, she got very angry. She was surprised when I suggested that a more direct form of communication was necessary. Had she gone into the house and said, "I need your help in the backyard "and had he then refused, her anger would at least have come out of a direct communication.

If couples worked as hard at telling the truth about their feelings, as they do at trying to get around the truth, marriage would be revolutionized. Remember honesty and reality are the same. A deep level of intimacy cannot occur without being accurately tuned-in to each other's emotional wavelength.

It is less threatening to your spouse to report to him/her what your child is feeling than it is to accuse and condemn him/her. When you condemn, you are setting a judgment on your spouse, which may or may not be truth. The condemnation is up for debate. But when you report the feelings of your inner child there is no room for debate. You and only you know what you really feel. (That is, if you are stating an emotion) If you say, "I feel like what you are doing is cruel, awful, crazy" then you are not stating a feeling, you are judging. But if you say, "I really feel frightened, confused and angry when you act like that "you are stating feelings.

When we hear and report our inner child's feelings, our child is being cared for, protected and loved. Feeling secure in a marriage has more to do with our inner child's trust in us than it does with our trust in our spouse. "I am yours, truly." means telling the truth about what our child is feeling.

Courtship generally begins with a feeling and often ends when that feeling is gone. The feeling leaves for various reasons.

One reason is that the inner child does not get protected and well represented. Often feelings hurt and not reporting those feelings, and dealing with the issue behind the hurt, lead to anger. Anger is to romantic feelings what water is to fire. Hopefully we can love our spouse and be angry at the same time, but our emotions do not allow for sexual or romantic feelings and anger, at the same time. These feelings may alternate rapidly but they cannot be felt at the same time. If we want these feelings to return to the relationship then we must learn from, and process, our anger. Since anger generally comes from hurt, by taking care of our hurt inner child in the relationship, we can open the way for good feelings to return. Forgiveness means the angry feelings are gone - we are finished with the problem. Continuing to pout and seek revenge means we want the other person to hurt the way we are hurting. Understanding and caring for the inner child is the key to resuming a romantic relationship.

**The feel of love can't remove the risk**

A healthy balance between protecting and releasing our inner child in a relationship allows the feel of love to flow. We can't stop children from playing just because they get hurt. Getting hurt occasionally goes along with being a child. Getting hurt occasionally goes along with being loved.

## Hanging In there

Letting our partner love us means that we are not overprotecting our child. Often in broken relationships, I have found that one person has taken his or her inner child and gone into another room, or run away. The old song that says, "By the time I get to Phoenix she'll be rising, she'll find the note I left hanging on her door "tells of a man who takes his child and runs away from home. Letting myself be loved means I stay at home enjoying the good times, and embrace my inner child and love him during the bad times. That way my child self is always loved. Loving my child must include allowing my child to be loved.

## The gift of love

Loving someone means creating occasions for his or her pleasure, joy, and well being. The natural love of a child that flows through to our partner is what we experience as spontaneous love. When we hug, we give and get pleasure at the same time. To refuse to embrace our partner is as costly to us as it is to our partner. Our love becomes confused. Love by nature is supposed to give. When it is not giving, then something feels wrong. To tell a child he cannot hug his mother or father, or that he cannot buy them presents for their birthdays or for Christmas, would be cruel to a child. When we withdraw the gifts of affection or other gifts from someone we love, we are being cruel to our inner child.

Certainly it is proper for us to give to, and do for, the one we love without needing to derive any benefits. It is okay for us to be totally unselfish in our efforts to make life better for them. I'm not sure it's possible to love this way for any extended amount of time, without something returning in kind - but I say, "Go ahead!" it's worth a try simply because we love them.

I read about a couple that was extremely competitive with each other. The competition rivaled who could out love and out give the other. They would hide gifts and cards in cabinets, drawers and each other's things with notes that read, "See, I love you more." This was a game in which the child in each could delight.

## VI -- God

Children often converse about God and with God as if they are already acquainted. That same familiarity is true with our inner child. That's why I have included this section about God. Since a relationship with God is personal, these personal feelings of anger, appreciation, complaint, and the like, also, describe our relationships with God. Just as parental direction and care are necessary' in relationships with persons, they also are needed in relationships with God. The role of the inner mother and father is to provide their child with support, love and understanding as a mirror of God. Consequently, the channels of communication with God will remain open for the inner child.

### Regression

"Whoever shall not receive the Kingdom of God as a little child, he shall not enter." Mark 10:15

When a baby takes his parent's finger and holds on, he may simply be carrying out a natural response. But within that natural response is the seed of a faith that responds to things that are bigger and stronger and able to help. Gradually as the child matures, less and less faith in his parents is needed because he learns to take care of himself. In fact, his education, skills and financial ability may go beyond that of his parents. Regressing in their presence may be of little or no value.

However, being childlike in the presence of God remains necessary' throughout life. We mature in learning, wisdom, understanding and the ability to care for our daily needs. And, we can vastly deepen our knowledge of God. But, if we ever lose our childlike awe and wonder, if we lose the romance of a God who watches over all, then we miss the joy and meaning of our faith just as we miss the joy and meaning of marriage without a sense of romance.

Therapy may be required in this area also. If we regress to bad religious experiences, then we will experience childlike fear of discomfort in any attempt to relate to God. For example: Carol reported that her grandfather, who molested her, also held her in a chair and forced her to read the bible.

It is ultimately up to our adult inner parents to mature to a healthy understanding of God and then embrace the inner child with the new understanding until the old sick feelings are gone. Our relationship to God should be pleasant.

**Dependence**

"When I become a man, I put away childish things." I Corinthians 13:11

Remaining "only" a child to God means a serious limitation on the relationship. I heard a minister once say, "If my child came to me in her adult years and said, 'Daddy, I have no will, no desire, no ambition, no interest apart from yours, I will do nothing unless you tell me to 'then I would consider myself a failure as a father."

Faith in God must be understood in the light of God's faith in us. Our freedom to choose is representation of God's faith in us. Our ability to love is dependent on our free will, because love is a choice.

The paradox of relating to God is that, although we are totally dependent on God - we must take full responsibility for ourselves. The inner child looks both to the inner parents and to God for love, care, protection and provision; however, the inner parents do not presume upon God to provide food without working, education without study, a wife without dating, or an appendectomy without seeking the aid of a surgeon. We are given the capacity to provide in ways, which require our effort. If we fail, we suffer consequences.

Being our own Mom and Dad is not replacement for God, it is affirming and accepting the God given capacity to be responsible for ourselves. We are not robots or puppets. Having the ability to make adult decisions, and to be responsible for those decisions, is the basis of our capacity to love. The closest we can be to inner harmony and peace is to accept God's love for us, to love God, and to love ourselves and others in a manner as close to God's unconditional love, as possible.

**Criticism and rejection**

"Nothing will ever be able to separate us from the love of God." Romans 8:39

Like a loving parent, God knows what will work and what will not work for his children and, of course He wants the best for them. If that comes off as critical and rejecting then you are likely projecting onto God the kind of parenting you received as a child.

To tell someone that God is like a father may distort the relationship if that person's father beat him, molested him, or was absent from him.

Recently, when a client was dealing with a

heavy, critical inner parent I placed a big black chair symbolizing this critical parent, directly in front of her. First, I said, "Imagine all of your shoulds, oughts, musts, - that you cannot live up to - coming from the chair." Immediately she said, "I see my father sitting there." "What if you tell him you can't live up to all his expectations," I asked. She began to cry and said, "But, then he would reject me and I would lose him." She looked at me as if a revelation had come over her and said, "You know, that's the way I relate to God."

"Grace" is a term often used to describe God's unconditional love. Understandably, 'grace' is a hard concept to comprehend when someone has experienced a bitter and cruel life. Without getting into a discussion of theology or of pain and suffering, let me speak from my experience as a therapist. Because of the suffering many clients have endured, they do not think of God as gracious or "grace-full." Later, however, during the healing process of therapy (as they verbalize their pain and discover ways to avoid future pain), they become more open to the possibility of a God of "grace." Finding acceptance, appreciation and warmth during therapy make the question, "Why did I suffer?" less important and opens the way to enjoy a loving God of "grace". This is to say that a fuller understanding of "grace' comes after one has experienced something of grace rather than attempting to understand it beforehand.

My regression group suggested that I title this book, "Go Toward Your Pain" because I am constantly urging them to do that. I informed them it was not an original idea. Jesus both taught and practiced going toward pain. It's hard to believe that in His most painful moment of rejection and criticism He said to His disciples, "My peace I leave with you." Buddha taught and felt his pain, as have most significant religious leaders. The only path to enlightenment involves both pain and peace.

God's Grace can be found in the inner capacity to be our own mother and father. An adult who is childish all his life will suffer greatly and never really know the fuller meaning of God's Grace.

## Communication

"groanings which cannot be uttered."
Romans 8:26

The depressed person often feels that he has lost the ability to communicate with people and with God. I have seen people so depressed they could not say a word. Their only communication was a slight nodding of the head. The hopelessness of depression often renders communication useless. On the other hand, feeling that someone is listening gives hope. Sometimes faith means not having to say a word. It is the silent assurance that we are in the company of someone who loves us.

Communicating with God must include the full representation of all our feelings. If a person feels hate for God but instead speaks of love, then the dishonesty will spoil attempts at feeling intimate with God. Being talked out of believing our negative feelings, by our well-meaning parents, can create a dishonesty, which may easily carry over to our relationship with God. God is secure. He can handle our feelings and our deepest negative secrets. When the inner parents try to hush their inner child from speaking his real feelings to God, they show their lack of faith and place serious limitations on their inner child.

Our effort to honestly communicate to God our true feelings, struggles, secrets, dreams and aspirations is called prayer.

## Receiving Love

"If you hardhearted men know how to give good gifts unto your children, how much more shall your Father in heaven give good gifts." Matthew 7:11

Receiving love from God is not unlike receiving love from another person. You graciously take it as a gift. No matter how good our instructions are to our children, if love is not felt by the children nothing else seems to really count. While love may defy a complete definition, it certainly includes being accepted and appreciated.

The person loved feels that he is important to the one loving.

Receiving gifts is easy for a small child. But some adults don't receive gifts well. People sometimes get confused and think they have to earn or deserve a gift in order to accept it. If that's true, it is not a gift, but rather it is a wage. I have offered to give money to people who would not receive it. I have offered to see people in therapy at no charge, who refused to accept it. In every case, it was because they felt they did not deserve such a gift.

There are parents who might not take food or money for themselves but if their children were hungry or needy would take it for them. A loving parent will let the inner child receive God's love. Somehow that does not feel quite as selfish.

The specific way in which God extends his love to us is through the people who love us. As stated earlier, we are born with a capacity to be our own mom and dad. Just as a loving parent gives his child the necessary tools to handle the world, God gives us the capacity to parent ourselves in order to handle the world.

**Giving Love**

And the King shall answer-"In as much as you have done it unto one of the least of these my brothers, you have done it unto me." Matthew 25:40

Just as love is a gift to be received, it is a gift to be given. Some people make love a wage they must earn, or a wage the person they love must earn. It is important to understand that love by nature can never be anything but a gift.

How do we give God the gift of love? First, love opens the door to intimacy. Love is first a choice, and that choice then opens the door to feelings of gratitude and a desire to be close and intimate. Love is not limited to a feeling, but feeling is certainly included in love. To allow a close feeling to God is one way of giving love.

Since our contact with God is sensed as spiritual, we can say we love Him as a prayer, but how we put our love into action may be difficult to understand. However, if we join God in His love for others, we in turn express love to God. There is such a good feeling in parents who witness someone else truly loving their children. Somehow they feel loved, too. As God extends His love to us through people, He also receives our love through people.

## CONCLUSION

The quality of life is based on the quality of our relationship to self, others and God. Each relatively depends on the other in order to have a balance of life. To ignore self is to ignore others and God. To ignore others is to ignore self and God. To ignore God is to ignore self and other.

When we acknowledge and care for ourselves, we are prepared to relate beyond ourselves. For mother-self, daddy-self and child-self to live in harmony and a bond of mutual love and care, offers the Inner security and well being to move beyond ourselves. Trusting within ourselves is the prerequisite for trusting outside ourselves.

That inner trust occurs when the inner parents fully adopt the child-self and the child-self lets them. A happy inner family does not require unrealistic bliss. The inner family, like all families, has their ups and downs. They disagree, argue, make up, celebrate and disagree again. All of this is a part of the maturing, growing process. Accepting the process can bring a reasonable peace. We will never perfect ourselves.

Accepting the inner family process will also allow

you to be more patient with relating to others. Having a warm close relationship with someone does not have to wait until all the problems are overcome. Otherwise intimacy would never occur.

This is also true of our relationship with God. If you wait until you are morally and spiritually perfect before you attempt a relationship with God, there will never be a relationship with God. Certainly God is aware of this, that's why He/She offers us unconditional acceptance. Otherwise we would never know Him/Her.

Life is supposed to work. If it is not working for you that does not mean you should never have been born, or that you are no good, or that your circumstance in life cannot be changed. Since you are already here, you are supposed to be here and have purpose and meaning in your life. As a person, you carry the same value as all other people; and, as long as you are alive, if you want, change is always possible.

I have offered to you a method of identifying your: Inner mother and father and child-selves not as a simple solution to complex problems, but as a practical approach to something that will help make life better for you amidst the confusion, problems and struggle.

Inner harmony provides peace, security and love which fills life with meaning, purpose and joy. You can do it.

M Tatum